MW00458810

Once Upon a Lifetime

Lolita J. Frederick-Harris

TORCH RUNNER
PUBLICATIONS

Dedicated to:

*My children and grandchildren, who have my forever love
and gave me a reason to write this book.*

*My husband, Stephen Harris, who patiently allowed me the time
and gave me encouragement to hang in there!*

Many friends who have encouraged me.

The memory of women who have greatly influenced my life:
Vonitta F. Gurney Boylan
Rosella J. Yoder
Barbara Edwards
Jean Darnall
Roberta Harris
Tella Muñoz

My sweet friend, Michelle Merriman, who consented to edit this.

*The Memory and Life of Dr. Phillip Michael Frederick,
absent, but never forgotten.*

*"…I will pour my Spirit on your descendants, And
my blessing on your offspring." Isaiah 44:3*

Contents

Introduction

"Trust in the Lord with all your heart, and lean not unto your own understanding. In all your ways acknowledge Him, and He will direct your paths." Proverbs 3:5-6

Why in the world would I write a book? What could possibly be interesting enough about my life that anyone would waste their time reading about it? But there are several of you out there who have asked me to do this and seem to think I might have something to say, so this is really all your fault...be it good or bad! On the other hand, I realize how clearly God has spoken to me, nudged (pushed?) me, or comforted me through the hearing of others' walks with Him. If somehow this can serve that purpose for a few, then I will be blessed. "No one is an island unto himself..." and what serves as experience to one person, often becomes second-hand wisdom for another. I have chosen to sprinkle Bible verses in here and there; these verses are from among my favorite ones and I trust they will encourage you as well. (Verses will be from the NKJV.)

I believe I can safely say that I was the last generation of missionary kids raised by the truly pioneer missionaries of a now nearly forgotten era. This in and of itself gives me a rather unique set of experiences. In those long-ago days, missionary work was not a short-term adventure to add to one's résumé, but rather a life-long commitment, regardless the cost...and cost it most often did. MK's (Missionary Kids) are also known as TCK's (Third Culture Kids), because they often feel they don't belong here, there or anywhere. But then, this world is not my home anyway, so I adjust just fine wherever, thank you very much!

So here it is, and – kind of like me – what you see is what you get! But aren't you glad that God can take the ordinary details of your life and make them into consistent miracles in His hands? When we look back over our lives and see the unique, amazing pattern He has designed for our own special tapestry, our hearts thrill with thanksgiving over what is past and with even greater expectations for the future as we wait on Him. As the Psalmist says in Psalm 130:6, *"My soul waits for the Lord, more than those who watch for the morning..."*

Please bear in mind, this is not intended to be a real book – much less a literary work; it is intended to be a fireside chat (or pool side, depending on the season when you read it!) among friends who have one great thing in common: we love the Lord, love His kids, and are eager to encourage one another.

My greatest wish is that my children and grandchildren will read it, in hopes that they will then better understand the crazy lady in their life who is their mother, mother-in-law, grandmother, or great-grandmother, whichever the case may be. I certainly am no wonder woman...but I am sure I have made them wonder about me many times! They are the joy of my life, my truly greatest accomplishment. Brenda, Leahna, Debra and Rebecca – I love you dearly. Denny, Don, Terry and Jesse – you are just as much my boys as if I had raised you. And to the world's most gorgeous, intelligent and amazing grandchildren and great grandchildren...mine, of course...my heart swells when I think of you, and you daily fill me with awe, new thrills and high hopes for the future. You are my message to the future, and I know for certain that you are a good one!

· I ·

It's a Girl!

"When a newborn opens its tiny fist and clutches its father's finger for the first time, the man is entrapped for life."

My parents, Charles Edwin Gurney and Vonitta Fern McCarthy, met at the Foursquare Gospel Church in Woodburn, Oregon in 1938, on the first day my mother attended the church upon moving to Woodburn from Wyoming. She was fifteen. Born in Wyoming, she had remained there with her grandmother to finish the high school year as her parents, Dan and Minnie McCarthy moved to Oregon. They hoped to improve their lot and seek better weather due to the illness of their younger daughter, Mary Alice, who unfortunately passed away not long after their move.

My mother was a beautiful, young, spunky brunette, with dark eyes inherited from her Irish father. Since the age of seven, she had been a child preacher with the Pentecostal Church of God. My father was seventeen. He had grown up in Woodburn where my grandparents, Charles and Ella Gurney, owned the most popular grocery store in the area.

He was tall, blonde, blue-eyed, handsome, athletic, and owned his own car in high school, quite a badge of honor and cause for popularity in those days. From that first meeting, their future was pretty much sealed...he literally fell for her...as he entered the church and headed to meet her, he tripped and fell down in the aisle at her feet!

In 1941, they headed for L.I.F.E. Bible College in Los Angeles, California, and became engaged. They were married on Sunday evening, February 14, 1943, in a filled-to-capacity Angeles Temple, by Aimee Semple McPherson, founder of the Foursquare movement. My mother was the class speaker at their graduation in February of 1945, and by then I was on the way. I always say I was nearly born on a church platform...which could very easily have happened!

Following their graduation, they left for Ohio to pastor a little church (key word here being little!) and I was born not long after, on May 5, 1945, in Lodi, Ohio. Please keep in mind, they were pastoring a church where things were very tight financially. On one occasion my Daddy mentioned to the ushers, as they were counting the offering, that he just didn't see how they were going to make it. The usher was Johnny-on-the-spot with an answer, "You know Brother Gurney, the more you put in, the more you will get out!" This, to the pastor who would mail in a postage stamp to the district office to cover the amount of tithes the church needed to submit!

Money being as scarce as it was, the few birth announcements they could afford upon my birth were waiting to be filled in with the baby's name and statistics and sent to relatives and close friends. Well, my father said he wanted a little girl, she would be blonde, she would sing, and she would be named Lolita...and as my mother labored to bring me into the world, he sat in the waiting room and filled out the birth announcements with my name! I have always been very grateful – for his sake – that I was a girl, or he would have been in major trouble.

I don't have many memories of Ohio, as I was only about eighteen months old when my parents began to hit the road as evangelists. But I do remember the windows at the front door of the church for some reason. And over the years I heard a few details about the area from a boy my parents procured legal custody of while they were there. Gary Black was twelve years old at that time and until the day he passed away, he called me "Tita Doll" (Tita being how I first said my name). When my parents began traveling, my McCarthy grandparents opened their home for him to live with them. My grandpa had a dream that he was fulfilling, taking in needy boys (ages eight through high school) and raising them in a good home environment while instilling in them strong work ethics and Christian principles. Gary was a life-long fan of mine and proud as a peacock of anything I did. I miss him.

Although the memories are scarce from that era, I do know I must have been greatly loved. I have never felt insecure in my life and I know it was due in great part to the early years when I was loved, spoiled and made aware of my value as a person. Don't get me wrong – I wasn't spoiled in the "rotten" sense…just spoiled because I was so cute, talented and precocious!

****

After leaving Ohio to become evangelists, we would spend a little time between "gigs" in Oregon visiting

13

my grandparents, the Gurneys, and often staying at my McCarthy grandparents' home. They lived on a farm, and there was always a never-ending list of possibilities for me to have fun. Some of them were fun for me – not for others, and some ended up not being fun for me either. Let me just give you a few examples…

My grandparents raised some rabbits, and I would watch as they were fed little pellets that they called rabbit seeds. Well, one day my grandma found me digging little holes in the middle of her garden and "planting" the pellets. I told her I was going to grow rabbits too! I also picked the peppercorns out of baloney and was found planting them. I loved baloney (still do), and since they grew about everything we ate, I thought I would just add variety to our provisions. OK – so I was only three or four then – give me a break!

Not too far from the main farmhouse, there was a pump house. It was always cool in the pump house in the summertime, so my grandma would keep the abundant supply of fresh fruit there. Unfortunately, there was also an abundance of bees in and around the pump house. I had been warned of this and told NOT to ever go into the pump house. To my detriment, nature being what it is, that was exactly where I would find myself wanting to go. One day I got up the courage, sneaked over to the pump house and opened the door to get an apple only to be met by a swarm of bees that must have realized I was terribly sweet! I started crying like some wild critter, Grandma came running to rescue me, and took me into the house to nurse my bee stings. She never said, "I told you so," she only said, "I hope you have learned your lesson!" I had. And to this day I am a respecter of bees.

During picking season, all the boys and any other able, willing, workers would be in the orchard picking cherries and peaches. Grandpa had long tables made of boards and saw-horses set up in the orchard to place the buckets of fruit on as it was picked and distributed into the baskets that would be taken to market. Being too short to pick and having no one to pay me attention, I proceeded to climb up on the table and put on a singing and dancing routine over, around, through and in the fresh fruit. Unfortunately, Grandpa did not think it was a good show at all.

****

I fondly remember one Christmas we spent there. My beloved Aunt Rosella (my mother's younger sister who I adored) and Gary were both attending a Christian high school, and their class was putting on a big Christmas musical. They decided they would take me as part of the entertainment. I still remember prancing on top of the baby grand piano dressed to perfection by my grandmother's seamstress talents, while singing favorite Christmas songs like, *Here Comes Santa Claus, Santa Claus is Coming to Town,* and *Frosty the Snowman.* Then the three of us sang *White Christmas,* with me singing the melody and Rosella and Gary playing the piano in duet and harmonizing. We brought the house down, and I was the star of the show that night!

Gary had a horse; it had an almost perfect star on its forehead and was named Fairy (as in Fairy Godmother) and I loved Gary to take me for rides. I was around four at the time, and it was quite an organizational feat to fit in a ride between my eating ALL my lunch, his school/work schedule, my nap time, and Grandma's idea of what was a good time for such a ride. One day in particular stands out in my mind. We had just saddled up after lunch and were on our way down the road when I said to Gary, "The worst thing would happen! I have to go potty!" Being practical, he said we would just ride back, I could take care of the matter and we would start our ride over again. But I knew how that would end. "If we do, Grandma will make me take a nap now!" And she did.

****

One of my antics I am sure my mother never forgot was a day I climbed up in the hayloft of the barn. Climbing up was easy – I just could not get down! My mother was on her way to speak at a church that evening and could not find me to say good-bye. Of course she panicked, and I could hear her calling my name all over the place. I finally yelled out that I was in the hayloft. She came marching over to the barn and commanded me to come down immediately, to which I tearfully responded that I couldn't. She kept saying, "Of course you can! You got up there alone, didn't you?" Well yes, I got up there alone, but that was the end of my ladder abilities. She finally started to climb the ladder to get me, high heels, little straight skirt, and dark eyes flashing! We both got down safely, but not before my grandpa appeared, laughing heartily at the sight.

But I also want you to know I worked hard in that old farmhouse. Grandma was meticulous in keeping the well-weathered wooden floors waxed to perfection. She would apply the wax during the day, and when my aunt and all the boys got home from school, it was their job to shine the floors. They would have me lie down on a big towel and then swing me around on the floor in a circular motion to shine the floors. I did come in handy! Those are good memories that were thrown in between the traveling times.

My Gurney grandparents were also hard-working people, mostly all business, unless I was there to interrupt their disciplined schedules. I could always count on candies and ice-cream from the store when I visited, my favorite being Big Hunk and Mountain Bar candy bars. Later, as a teen, I thoroughly enjoyed playing "storekeeper" for short times. Grandma Gurney was usually pretty prim and proper (being of English background) but I could always get just about anything I wanted from Grandpa Gurney (who was of French lineage).

· II ·

The Formative Years

"If you make sure a child asks Jesus to be Master of their life,
you can be sure that child will be the captain of their future."

My earliest memories are not of playgrounds, picnics or parties. I remember things like church pianos, Sister Lydia's cat scratching me when my parents left me in her care while they went on "visitation," revival meetings, laying down in church on a real padded pew for the first time (as compared to hard wooden ones I was accustomed to), practicing a new song for the next meeting, and hanging on to railings while I sang because the platform was so high I would get dizzy when I tried to see over it. I remember "photo shoots," to have my picture taken for advertisement purposes.

And I remember traveling – a lot! When my parents hit the road as evangelists, I was the soloist for the meetings (I began singing at age three) and was known as "The Sweetheart of Revival." (For some reason, my husband Mike was honestly very proud of that and kept one of the old flyers on his desk.) As I mentioned, my grandmother

McCarthy was an accomplished seamstress, and I had a special outfit to wear that matched the particular song I would sing...a cowgirl outfit for, "A Christian Cowgirl"; a red, white and blue outfit for, "God Bless America"; a sailor outfit for, "Ship Ahoy"; a very fancy dress for, "The Holy City"; and others I don't remember. I was a very well-dressed sweetheart!

We pulled a small vacation trailer behind an older Ford from church to church, holding revival meetings in the evenings. Till this day I am not very fond of raisins, because Mommy decided those little boxes were handy, healthy snacks as I rode along. I found all kinds of things to do with them...eat them, smash them, put them in my ears, up my nose, even between my toes. A girl has to keep entertained somehow! And of course, endless coloring books (complete with melted crayons in the summertime), and always the all-important doll and stuffed animal. Mine was an elephant named Gopey.

During one of our stops my mother developed shingles. When she didn't show up for the evening meeting, one of the ladies told me she heard my mother was ill and asked what she had. "She has roofs," was my reply. Shingles/roofs...made sense to me!

At some point we acquired a new Nash Rambler. Daddy got to see it roll off the assembly line. We no longer pulled a trailer, as the most noteworthy feature of the new car was that the front seats folded all the way flat with the back seats to make a full-size bed. I remember the three of us sleeping there many nights as we saved on lodging bills. We basically lived in that car. I guess people would consider us underprivileged to have to live like that; I thought it was magnificent! Laying in the cramped quarters between my parents, looking out the windows at the twinkling stars, was the utmost feeling of security. I have been blessed throughout my life to sleep well, wherever I might be...and that has included a lot of places! *"I will both lie down in peace, and sleep; for You alone, O Lord, make me dwell in safety."* Psalm 4:8.

I can still remember the excitement of pulling into yet another church and parsonage complex to see the pastors and find out if they had kids (usually not, at least not anywhere near my age), and if it was a big church or little one. In my mind I could generally determine how prosperous the revival would be financially by that first glimpse of the parsonage. My parents never asked me, but if money had been what they were looking for, I could have saved them a lot of hard work – we could have just kept on going to check out the next place until I spotted the signs of bigger offerings!

****

When I was five, my parents decided to pioneer a church in Dallas, Oregon. We lived in the church basement with fake windows: my mother hung framed pictures and put curtains over them, while my father put lights up under the curtains to make it look like daylight was shining in. It is amazing how small things can make such big impressions. When I've been faced with challenges to making our own home comfortable over the years, in numerous and dubious places, I always remember that little basement home and knew that if my mother managed to make it feel so comfortable and homey there, it could be done anywhere with a little imagination and work. "Creativity is the God-given ability to take something ordinary and make it into something special," (Emilie Barnes). Hopefully, I have instilled some of that same ingenuity in my own daughters. In my mind that was always a special place.

A few years ago we took my mother...ninety-two at the time...to revisit Dallas and take a few pictures at the old church. The reality of how much they had sacrificed hit me hard as I got down on my knees to peek in the just above ground basement window of my old bedroom. (Interestingly, Steve and Nancy Harris pastored that same church twelve years later...more about them further on.)

It was in that basement home that I told Mommy I wanted to ask Jesus into my heart. I might have been young, but it was real – and it is still real today! *"Train up a child in the way he should go, and when he is old he will not depart from it."* Proverbs 22:6.

We later moved into an honest-to-goodness house in Dallas, and the Christmas we spent in that house is among my most cherished memories. Daddy made me a wonderful record player and play stove and I got a new doll. Talk about hitting the jackpot! We didn't stay in Dallas too long, but while we were there I was baptized, by my Daddy, in the Pacific Ocean along the Oregon coast. Trust me, with water that cold, a baptism is an unforgettable experience!

Following close on my own baptism was the baptism of a little puppy I had been given. The Reverends Elmer and Jean Darnall came to Dallas for a revival. They had been my parents' very special friends since college. (My middle name is Jean after her, and their son John's middle name is Edwin, after my father.) It was only logical that two preacher's kids would play preacher games – thus my poor puppy's baptism. A few days later said baptism was exceeded by our anointing it with oil for healing when it came down with influenza, no doubt caused by a too-long immersion in cold water. But it did survive. It got to be pretty big to live in a basement and ended up being adopted by a family in the church that had a big farm.

****

When I was close to six, my parents were asked to go pastor another larger church. We were going to settle down, enroll me in school and be really normal, in Seattle, Washington. At that time I made my first major purchase with my own money earned from singing at special events: a Chihuahua puppy I named Chico. I don't remember much about Seattle except that it rained a lot and was really cold the winter we were there. We made some good friends; there were two single ladies in the church who vied for my attentions through showering me with gifts and fun outings, so I was quite content there. It was from them that I received a Mickey Mouse watch, one of the earliest made. I started to school and we lived in a nice parsonage, but it was to be short-lived.

My parents' desire had always been to go to the mission field, so when the call came for them to go before the Foursquare Mission Board in Los Angeles, we set off on an exciting train trip to California in February 1952. My permanent mental photo flashes of California are still based on that first introduction to the Southern California countryside while racing down the train tracks from Washington... palm trees, bright flowers, immense fields – and warm weather with no rain! Although I was vaguely aware that our life was about to change somehow, I had no idea how greatly this change would affect my entire life. Leaving grandparents, Aunt Rosella and her husband Wayne, Uncle Percy and his wife Charlene, Aunt Lou and her husband Ben, really didn't sink in for a while. It was as though the entrance into the magical California landscape was a foretelling of the amazing life I was to live from then on. *"For I know the thoughts that I think toward you, says the LORD, thoughts of peace and not of evil, to give you a future and a hope."* Jeremiah 29:11.

Then it was back to Seattle to pack and leave for Panamá on my first airplane trip, something I am positively hooked on to this day. On any given day, if someone offers to fly me anywhere, I take it as divine direction and start packing! Although I have been on some pretty hair-raising flights, I've never been scared off from flying – no fear! I figure it this way: if I'm on a flight and through whatever incident am suddenly heaven bound, I am just that much closer to my final destination!

****

Panamá – what a far cry from Seattle! The strong impressions made on my young mind still spin in a kaleidoscope of colors, smells and sights. The rich tropical vegetation, strange foods, unknown fruit juices forced upon me when water was not a drinkable option, and curious people everywhere. It was in Panamá that I first experienced the dubious joy of actually sleeping in a hammock – all night. Who would have ever guessed that years later I would have a child born in the very place of my first missionary experience, in the city of Colón! While in Colón, we stayed with missionaries Claude and Juanita Updike. We also spent considerable time with missionaries Leland and Barbara Edwards, who I fell in love with and later became my second parents.

Since singing was my contribution to the ministry, I now had to learn new songs in a new language. I remember listening very closely to people as they talked, watching their eyes and hands, trying to imagine what they were saying. At first, it was intimidating...almost scary...to hear the strange sounds and watch as people actually responded to them. But it slowly became utterly fascinating to me and I loved the sing-song lilt of their voices. It wasn't long before I began to understand certain words and phrases. That only made me yearn to understand more.

Thus began my passionate connection with the language that would eventually become my best-loved means of communication. Soon I was singing in Spanish and trying out my ability to converse with other children. How exciting to realize that they actually understood me! I would lie on my cot (wherever in Panamá we happened to be) and practice words until I fell asleep. I mastered the tongue-rolling for double "rr", the strange "ñ" sound, and even the sing-song way in which words were put together.

One of my most impressive memories of Panamá was a trip we made to somewhere in the interior (Bocas del Toro, I believe) for meetings. We were to be fed there, and some ladies were cooking a big pot of chicken soup out on an open fire that was low to the ground. As I stood outside the church building watching them go about their cooking, a dog came over to the pot, grabbed a chicken leg that was sticking over the top, and pulled the whole chicken out and started to run off with it. A lady caught the dog, retrieved the chicken, and threw it back into the pot. I remember thinking how fast she was and how quickly she solved the problem. It never occurred to me to question the sanitation issues involved with that solution!

It was during this period that Mommy also became my schoolteacher. I don't recall there being any disciplined time scheduled for learning, but vividly recall learning to read and write out things on my own. Daddy was my personal math instructor, and all his teachings were of a practical nature. This pretty much spoiled me, as when I later was in "real school," unless math had a practical reason, I wanted nothing to do with it. I loved to read; learning – just about anything – became my constant companion and close friend. I am still an avid reader and can go through a full book in a matter of hours.

I particularly developed a great interest in seeing how people lived, how they went about their daily tasks, what utensils were used in their homes, how they dressed and how they related to each other. I had no idea I was majoring in cultural anthropology at the time!

My music class became the music that drifted through the trees and streets of the villages and cities we visited and instilled in me an appreciation for any and all types of music. (My collection today includes everything from Celtic to rumba, tango to rock, classical to country). I didn't realize it then, of course, but this quest for studying people and cultures would serve me well throughout my life. I have loved people from a very early age...all people, all races, all cultures.

****

After some three months in Panamá, the mission team my parents were a part of moved on to the next place of thrill and intrigue for me, Bluefields, Nicaragua, an island just off the Nicaraguan coast. The small hotel where we stayed, in retrospect, must have been a replica from the "Casa Blanca" movie set. My days involved drinking coconut milk, eating turtle soup, turtle steak, turtle hamburgers, turtle stew, and anything else turtle, sleeping under mosquito nets, visiting and singing at the schools and getting a lot of attention from everyone on the island. A little blonde girl was a novelty in itself; one who sang was even more so.

It was here that my parents thought I had been kidnapped. The hotel maid who was supposed to watch over me after I would sing in the outdoor evening services, decided one evening to take me for "show-and-tell" to her friends and relatives. After our visiting expedition, she took me back to the hotel and put me to bed, right where I belonged. I later discovered that my parents had been frantically searching everywhere for me, as were a great number of other people, including the island police.

It was also here that I saw my father do a wild dance on the platform as he preached...at first, I thought it was the "spirit" moving him, although he was usually pretty reserved, and I wondered about it. But as the sermon and the hip-hopping continued, I began to notice that as he would do his two-step, a small little lizard would drop off his leg or down his shoe. I then realized his dance was an attempt to keep the little critters from climbing up his legs!

I clearly recall a day in July 1952, when I heard a radio news station reporting the death of Eva Perón, first lady of Argentina, wife of Juan Domingo Perón. I had no idea where in the world Argentina was, had never heard of her before, and did not hear of her again until years later; but on that day I felt an intense sadness and tears stung my eyes as I felt sorry for the people of Argentina. I still see myself on that day, walking along a sidewalk with our hotel maid/nanny and hearing the news report being loudly played over the radio of the little pulpería (small neighborhood grocery store) as we walked by. I have thought about this incident so many times over my life, and the strange impact it made on me. I truly believe that even at that early age, God was preparing me to minister in Argentina with a compassion that I had literally grown up with. *"Ask of me, and I will give you the nations for your inheritance and the ends of the earth for your possession."* Psalm 2:8.

Following a time of six weeks in Bluefields, we headed further up into Central America. San Jose, Costa Rica was our first stop, for only a very few days. San Jose was a bit more sophisticated than our previous stops. It was there that I was introduced to jewelry...an intoxication I have never overcome (much to my husbands' dismay)! My Daddy bought me a silver necklace with little rosettes around it and a real turquoise bead in the middle of each rosette. I remember my mother telling Daddy he was starting a bad thing, and his response, "If that is her worst addiction, I think we are pretty safe!"

Managua, Nicaragua, was our next stop, another cultural change. Here, the surroundings were much more boisterous and grimy, city life with a touch of the tropical splendor of Panamá and the island. It now amazes me that as a child I could perceive so many nuances in each of these locations – but I did. Each place presented me with new playthings that caught my parents' fancy and soon ended up in my little tote bag that I carried everywhere.

Perhaps my favorite memory from our stop in Managua is of me sitting on a park bench while a little ebony-skinned shoeshine boy polished my white shoes. I have remembered that moment many times and always been overwhelmed by the smiling, happy face of a lad who had to work hard at such a young age, yet did so happily and willingly, and the sense that no matter where we are from, what our station in life, our skin color or of what nationality we are, God's amazing love extends to us all and gives us each joy in serving in the ways He has planned for us.

We remained in Managua for a couple of weeks as my parents surveyed the possibilities of starting a church there. Then we moved on to Honduras where, ultimately, we made our home.

Tegucigalpa, the capital, was a beautiful quaint colonial city with very narrow streets, nestled in a small valley surrounded by pine-tree covered hills. It was the city I would grow up in. The huge cathedral and central plaza fascinated me, and my favorite pastime was to walk block after block with my father as he surveyed the city. May I just say, my father was six feet tall, and most of those six feet seemed to be legs; he walked fast! So, he walked while I ran.

Our life there started out in hotels, another favorite habit I acquired. In my book, no hotel is too fancy or too plain; they just each have a flavor of their own and I enjoy them all. I am sure being waited on has a lot to do with it! The first hotel was the best in the city, very nice, up-scale. It was there I was introduced to consommé and thought I was quite sophisticated as I sipped the chicken broth.

From there we moved to a smaller local hotel, and although it was a much more humble, very simple, rather rustic hotel, I was given a lot more attention there!

After being at the hotel for a few weeks, my grandfather shipped my little Chihuahua to me. Following a three-week wait for her arrival, my parents painfully explained that she would probably never arrive or worse, be dead upon arrival. I prayed about that! The dog showed up in great shape, with an almost empty box of baby cereal sitting in a little slot my Grandpa had made inside the crate he had made with a note that said, "Feed one tablespoon twice daily, mixed with water. Please give fresh water often." A double dish for the cereal and water and a flannel blanket completed the dog's travel equipment. When she arrived, Chico immediately became everybody's mascot, especially after they heard about her amazing travel experience. She lived until I was eighteen!

****

In early November of 1952 my mother and I made a trip back to Oregon. My mother had found she was pregnant and since we had no house yet, it was decided we go to Oregon for her to see a doctor and get the necessary items needed for a new baby. This was all quite a miracle, as my parents had opted to adopt a child just prior to us leaving Seattle, but of course had to forgo that decision when we left. My mother says it must have been the oysters in Bluefields!

While we were gone, Daddy found rented lodgings for us and our shipment from the US arrived. Although by no means fancy quarters to most people, the fact that I had a real bedroom made me feel like a princess. No doubt subconsciously I realized, even then, how well off we were in comparison to those around us. The front of the building was a large room intended for a store, where we held church; behind it was a little sitting room, kitchen and patio, with two rooms and a bathroom upstairs where we had our bedrooms. The only draw-back was our next-door neighbor – or should I say, their pet. They had a huge macaw parrot, beautiful and excellent at imitating speech. Each morning at 6:00, Daddy would call from their bedroom, "Lolita, it's time to get up!" It wasn't too many mornings later that as soon as the sun would rise – early – the dumb parrot would yell in his crazy parrot voice, "Lolita, it's time to get up!" I never did like that bird!

Soon thereafter, we welcomed a baby brother into our home when Gerald Edwin was born on March 7, 1953. I was nearly eight and this new addition was a great excitement to me. I considered Gerry to be my own personal property that my mother had the job of caring for. I suppose, due to the age difference, to this day I feel very protective of him, even though he stands nearly a foot above me and is my fire-fighter hero!

****

When I finally entered the second half of second grade at the American School in Tegucigalpa, I knew I had arrived! Here I was able to have all those things I loved: learning in general, Spanish in particular, and a library full of books, just beckoning me to read them all, which I pretty much did…Nancy Drew, the Hardy Boys, and anything else in the library.

Although most of the educational hours spent there are somewhat of a blur, I still have contact with some of the kids I sat by and studied with. The student body was quite international in background, which added to my love of learning more about other cultures and practices. Every day my parents gave me the equivalent of a nickel in US money to buy a bottle of soda-pop to accompany my home-packed lunch. Hmmm…maybe the fact that I had one almost every day for lunch is why I am not a soda pop drinker today! That school may not have been the world's best, but it certainly instilled in me some good study ethics and made me realize the incomparable value of a bilingual education.

My favorite annual event was Honduras Independence Day, September 15th. All the schools got to march in a big city-wide parade, and I felt so important in my very proper dress uniform (which I still have), complete with hat and white gloves. I didn't think life could ever get much better, even though I was always exhausted at the end of the three-mile parade route.

· III ·

Learning the Ropes Firsthand

"Realize that life is a school and you are here to learn. Problems are simply part of the curriculum that appear and fade away like an algebra class; but the lessons you learn will last a lifetime."

If you want to be a missionary, there is no better way to know what you are getting into than being a missionary's kid – except, then you might decide you really don't want to be a missionary after all. But I will have to admit, I can't think of a more exciting childhood. Along with the new surroundings and a new baby brother came another great addition – a maid! Her name was Lydia, and she was a sweet young lady needing a place to live who quickly became my ally in most situations, not to mention the doting, jealous protector of my brother. I haven't a clue if she was a hard worker, but she was sure a great asset to have around.

The beginnings of the new church are vague in my mind; I do remember open air meetings in the vacant lot next to the rented building where we lived, with missionaries Claude and Juanita Updike joining to help with the opening revival meetings. I sang most every night. I know there were always a lot of people there and that my parents were very excited about it.

Following the series of outdoor meetings, the church building was opened and was filled each time the doors were opened. Of course, all the preaching my parents did was filtered through an interpreter, but obviously the message was getting through.

Next door to the church was a cantina; every time one of the inebriated customers saw us, they would attempt to say whatever English words they happened to know. Daddy was having quite a trial learning Spanish, and on one occasion, after a drunk had greeted us, I told Mommy I had a solution to Daddy's language problem...he should just drink some of that stuff those guys drank and he would be able to talk in Spanish!

I saw tremendous healing miracles, had the amazing privilege of watching peoples' lives change over days and weeks, and watched in awe as people of very poor, humble settings began to prosper not only spiritually and physically, but financially as well. We didn't have talented musicians, choirs or padded pews; my mother played an accordion, my dad and I sang, and the cheaply made hard wooden benches seemed extravagant to all of us at the time.

One night there was a lot of commotion as church was starting when a lady was taken out of a taxi and put into her wheelchair. Everyone seemed to know her...and rightfully so. She was the sister-in-law of the ex-president of Honduras and had been paralyzed for several years following a serious auto accident. At the end of that service my parents prayed for her, she got up out of the wheelchair and walked home! Her husband was with her the next night and shortly thereafter my parents were invited to ex-president Galvez's home and had the opportunity to give him the good news of the Gospel.

I remember some very large weddings in the vacant lot, because the church was too small to hold the people. I was the flower girl in all of them and many to follow until I became too old to fulfill that roll; then I became a bride's maid.

Having learned the language so quickly was not only fun for me, but a great advantage to my parents. I was able to translate at the market, the gas station, and even in church. I will never forget the first Mother's Day service, where my father was preaching on the "Blessedness of Motherhood," – only the interpreter, Chente, was preaching his own version, the "Blessings of the Hat of a Mother." Hood – hat – he just wasn't familiar with the term, "motherhood." I finally leaned over to my mother and said, "Mommy, I don't think Chente is getting it!" A quick aside took place between my parents, the interpreter and myself, and the sermon then continued in a more sensible vein.

It wasn't long before I started teaching a Sunday School class for the younger children – I was eight years old. I had very little long-term experience in any Sunday School classes due to all the traveling we did, but of course Mommy taught me Bible stories for as long as I can remember. However, when it came time for me to teach, I obviously needed to attend class first at home during the week in English with my mother, practice with the flannel graph board, then teach it in Spanish on Sunday. I soon discovered it wasn't so much fun as it was work! I don't know how much those little kids learned at Sunday School, but I know I learned a lot before I even got to the class.

The enjoyment of sharing what I had learned with others set into motion a principle that has been a motivating force in my life from then on. I have taught Sunday School, Bible Institute, seminars, women's groups, English, Spanish, Bible as Literature, gym, etiquette, cooking, wardrobe planning, university Spanish classes etc., etc., etc.... and I am still an avid student and teacher of whatever catches my interest.

My parents were both studying Spanish with a private teacher, an exhausting and time-consuming effort for them. Daddy did get to where he could preach and teach in Spanish, although he battled with the verbs and pronunciation all his missionary life. Sometime during 1953 my mother was to preach and had her notes all prepared in English, ready to use the interpreter. They both took the pulpit for her to preach, and then there was an interlude where she and Chente were discussing something. He sat down and she began to preach in Spanish! She later told us the Lord impressed upon her that she didn't need the interpreter; she was completely stunned, but she obeyed. Obviously, I don't remember the sermon. But at the time I was very surprised, and a little nervous, because I knew she didn't know that much Spanish; yet it was perfectly understandable. No one was more surprised than she was! She never used an interpreter again.

****

Along with the responsibilities of school and church activities, I had lots of time to make friends, discover new customs and foods, and play new games. My set of play dishes and pots and pans consisted of every size, shape and form of miniature pottery you can imagine, purchased for pennies at the local market. But not every kid was kind; I vividly remember being called, "Gringa de agua juca," which means "filthy water gringa." My parents told me not to pay attention, but after several successes at not paying attention, I had enough. The next time I was yelled at, I turned around and yelled back, "Y vos, indio de agua podrido!" ("And you, rotten water Indian!") I was reprimanded, of course, but felt a lot better! As I grew older, the boys still looked and commented, but much more pleasantly.

Nor was everything as fun as it looked. Two incidents in particular stand out in my memory as those what-not-to-do-for-fun things:

We rented the church/house from a gentleman who owned the building next door to us where he and his family lived and where he operated a large carpentry shop. (Years later I found myself reminiscing about those early years of church planting, and how appropriate that the carpenter's house we rented to be used to build The Carpenter's house!) Between his building and our rented building was the vacant lot used for open air services, and of course as a playground by day whenever the carpenter's children and I so decided. One of his daughters was my age and we became very close friends – we still keep in touch. However, he also had some sons who, like any normal boys, were full of orneriness and mischief.

Picture a group of three girls and two boys playing outside, running, skipping, tossing a ball; then one of the girls (me, of course) discovers these little piles of finely sifted dirt in assorted spots around the field. Once again that curious nature...I asked what these little dirt piles were.

One of the boys was quick to tell me that they had been softened and sifted for the express purpose of being able to sit in the soft, cool dirt without really getting dirty, and encouraged me to try it. Well, I did…and I will never forget the pain and agony of the stings from the fire ants or the anguish of my mother and our maid. The boys will never forget the punishment they received either!

My second ill-fated play-time adventure took place one afternoon when I was invited to play at the home of some people who attended the church. They had children in my age range, both boys and girls. When I arrived at their house, we all sat around the kitchen table and had sweet crackers and juice. In the middle of the table was a huge basket filled with these darling little elongated red things that really got my attention. I asked what they were (that curious nature again!) and one of the boys told me that their mom made face cream with them. If I would take some in my hands and rub them on my face it would feel wonderful and really make my skin look great. Well, I did. I can assure you, small roasted hot peppers are not good for your complexion!

****

I recall the first cross-country trip I made with Mommy in late 1953; we went by bus from Tegucigalpa to San Pedro Sula in the north. It was a very long, exhausting, arduous trip, and we were definitely an oddity on the crammed little bus, first receiving a lot of stares and then lots of questions. It was obvious that a foreign American lady with a little girl did not travel by that means very often! The bus broke down once and we all had to get out while they worked on it. I think the strongest memory that experience evokes was the extreme protectiveness I felt from my mother. I think she was more than a little frightened by the whole scenario, which translated into a strong concern for me. The trip took two days; we spent a night at the Missionary Aviation Fellowship compound in Siguatepeque, then continued the next day on a second bus.

In 1954 my parents were blessed to be provided with a four-wheel drive Willys Jeep. It was red and white, newly imported from the USA. That jeep took us literally everywhere in the country and soon became readily recognized in many towns and villages. I have had many cars at my disposal in the years since then, but the fondest memories I have of a car are of that one.

When I was around nine years old, I had an experience that would be etched in my mind for the rest of my life. It was a quiet Sunday afternoon, and Daddy decided to go to visit a young man who had been seriously injured in a bus accident. Of course, I wanted to go along. We drove out to the barrio in the Willys Jeep and parked as close as we could get to the row of small houses built up against a bank on a steep hill. I jumped out of the Jeep and just as Daddy came around and took my hand, we heard a door open and slam.

Looking around, we saw that a young man had come out of one of the houses and just at that moment put a gun to his head and shot himself. Daddy quickly turned me around and rushed toward the house where we were headed, but not before I saw the blood running down the sidewalk. I asked him why the young man would do that. I will never forget his answer: "Honey, he just must not have had any hope and hope is something you simply can't live without. That is why we need Jesus." As much as I remember seeing the suicide, the stronger image of that day was the sadness in my father's eyes and his never forgotten words… hope is something you simply can't live without. *"Show me your ways, O Lord, teach me your paths; guide me in your truth and teach me, for you are my God, my Savior, and my hope is in You all day long."* Psalm 25:4-5.

I am not sure about the dates, but I believe it was in 1954 that property was purchased for a church building. I do remember the excitement of my parents as they poured over plans, and I was always close at hand as Daddy measured the property and staked out the building. Many hours were spent as the church was being built and we all pitched in however we could. It was a grand celebration when the building was completed and the dedication service was held! The church is still prospering, and to me it will always be a monument to my parents' dedication and hard work.

(An interesting tidbit…a young man from Panamá, Victor Tejera, spent some time with us during the building program. He assisted with various church activities as well as with building projects. And now – sixty-five years later – we are attending the same church in Hesperia, California!)

In 1955, it was time for our first furlough, and to keep me on schedule for school, my parents sent me to the States before them so I could start the school year. I was ten years old and traveled alone! I had a plane change in Guatemala which, unfortunately, was 12 hours behind time. Daddy got in touch with Victor Tejera who was then living in Guatemala, so he came to the airport to entertain me. Between him and the meal tickets the airlines kept giving me every couple of hours, I had a great time! I arrived in Los Angeles to be picked up by my Aunt Lou, who immediately took me shopping for more modern clothes...cancan slip, longer dress, saddle oxfords...I think she might have been embarrassed by my little girl fashion! I spent a couple of days there before flying on to Oregon.

****

I was definitely a tom-boy! After about two and a half years in Tegucigalpa, we moved to a small residential area in the suburbs of the city where my parents felt it was much safer for us to grow up. Now I really felt like a princess! My greatest fun was riding my bike, swinging on ropes from trees Tarzan style (and receiving some serious rope burns on my hands more than once), building a clubhouse from the huge wooden crate (more like a small shed, really) that Daddy had built in the US to ship our belongings to Honduras in, and even hunting rabbits! You see, the only children my age in the neighborhood happened to be boys and, believe me, I strove to make true the words to the song, "Anything You Can Do, I Can Do Better!" I am sure I kept my poor mother in constant fear for my life; however, dear Lydia snuck me through various mishaps without ever worrying my mother about them.

The scars from falls, scratches, and bike accidents from those years are still imprinted on my various body parts, but the happy memories are also forever etched in my heart and mind. It was a wonderful, carefree, fun-filled childhood, and although I never had expensive toys, the bicycle given to me by a sweet lady in Oregon, the few real dolls my parents saved hard to buy for me, my pottery dishes, hand carved wooden toys from the market place, jacks and a deck of Mickey Mouse playing cards (I was a canasta shark!) were more than enough to keep me happy through my young years. The hula-hoop era gave me another means of showing off my talents, and it was quite an amazing thing to watch me get hoops going on hips, arms, neck and one leg...all at the same time!

Those childhood years were crammed with adventure and new experiences. I probably filled those years with more excitement and learning than most people put into a lifetime! There were open-air meetings when I would be singing and a tropical downpour would come, and I'd just keep "singing in the rain." Or the times a bug would fly in my mouth and I spat it out and kept on singing. Singing at weddings, singing at funerals, singing on the radio, singing indoors, outdoors, at church, at school...and I loved it.

And there was the thrill of seeing a blind child see for the first time upon being prayed for, people tossing aside their crutches, a remarkably large goiter on a lady's neck shrinking as we watched...God was constantly showing His power, and I was right there on the front row to see it. There is no way I could ever doubt God's grace, mercy and power.

· IV ·

Recognizing It's Not All Fun and Rejoicing

"There is nothing stable in the affairs of life; so don't get too excited over the good times nor too depressed over the bad!"

I also recall times when I would hear my parents agonizing over finances, difficulties in the work, and wishing they had more funds to help out in so many areas where people were needy. During those years, I was very naïve in the area of clothes. I felt fortunate to have shoes – one pair for play, one pair for dressy – and I knew the truly lovely clothes in my closet that my Mommy made for me were more than most families had for all of them together. It never occurred to me that I was missing out on the latest fads or fashions. Ignorance is truly bliss – and how unfortunate that it is no longer a commodity in most circles.

I will never forget my first Easter dress in Honduras. My brother was a baby and my mother was not up to sewing me a new dress or going with me to look for one, but she insisted I had to have an Easter dress. In that era, the only place to look was the big public market, so Daddy and

I went off on a shopping expedition. I may be wrong, but I believe this was the first time Daddy had every taken me shopping for a dress, and his store options were not very great! We finally found a little stall where the lady had a few cotton dresses in my size range, and I picked out not one, but two. The one I really loved was a brown print. Daddy had no idea, so he said they looked fine. When we got back to the house, I could tell Mommy was not too impressed… especially with the brown one…but they were Easter dresses to me and I wore them as proudly as if they had been from Macy's.

Although my parents loved and cared for us far and beyond what we would ever understand, there were times when duty called; they had to travel or be gone for a few days, and we would stay with Lydia. We missed them. I must admit jealousy got the best of me on more than one occasion, when I selfishly thought my Mommy should be where I wanted her to be when I wanted her to be; or Daddy would leave and not take me with him on one of the many trips he made into the interior of the country.

Whether good or bad, this is probably why I over-achieved to be there for my girls always, sometimes to the detriment of my own health and better judgment. During the time span when I had all four girls at home, one in high school, one in junior high, one in grade school and one in kindergarten, I attended every parent-teacher meeting (two for each child each semester…one English, one Spanish), every school play, musical presentation, open house, sports events, and whatever else happened to be going on…and my girls were VERY involved in everything! I don't know if it made any difference to them, but it sure made me feel good and felt like I was making up somehow for all the other things they might be missing out on by being raised as missionary kids (although they don't feel like they missed out on anything!). I love my girls beyond much.

Of course, there was also the flip side of all that: whenever Mommy or Daddy was gone for more than a day or two, they usually brought us back a gift. And the ULTIMATE compensation came once when Daddy traveled to the USA and brought me back an LP of Pat Boone's Greatest Hits and "Noxema" face cream. Life was good! The only concern was on my mother's part; she wasn't sure I should be listening to the worldly music. Little did we all know Pat Boone would eventually become an elder in a Foursquare church!

A memorable trip was one we made to the north coast of Honduras where the United Fruit Company had its operations. They had a commissary there that we somehow were able to get into, and I was allowed to buy a pair of blue jeans. I have always had a little bit of "country" in me, and I loved those jeans – even if I could only wear them at home when nobody else was around – nice girls did not wear pants in Honduras in that era!

I know we seldom took a vacation; maybe a day trip to a park or such, but that was it. However, we did take a beach vacation once, and both my brother and I loved the sand and sea. That short family vacation initiated my love for the seaside. I love simply sitting on the shore, watching the waves and hearing them crash on the beach. To me, that is pure relaxation.

Growing up in Honduras, we had our own particular favorite snacks, mainly fruit: mamones, guanabanas, zapotes, nances, guayabas, maranones, tamarindo (in a drink), bananas (called guineos), of which there were many varieties...butucos, shorter, fat ones; dátiles, little finger sized; manzanos, medium size sweet ones that almost tasted like apples; and the cooking ones, platanos, which we would fry up and eat like chips; and my favorite (rice) drink, horchata. We also ate a lot of mangos, our favorite being green ones with salt and pepper. I snatched salt and pepper shakers more than once from the house, then with my friends would go climb up a mango tree and sit in the branches eating the green fruit. Special treats were the little boxes of Chiclets, which contained two squares of gum, and of course the ice cream wagons with their variety of popsicles and ice creams. Another favorite were pupusas, little meat pockets that originated in El Salvador, and yuca con chicharrones...these two latter ones sold by sidewalk vendors and were on the Do Not Buy list, according to my mother. Sorry, Mommy!

Christmas was always special, thanks to my mother's ingenuity and my father's close over-sight of a very tight budget. Even then I had a sense of the sacrifice they were making, and Christmas mornings were the most special time of the year, just being together, a tree like no other tree in the entire neighborhood (universe, in my mind), stockings stuffed with candy, oranges, apples (a real treat), and nuts (also a big deal). And there were always gifts; I still wonder how some of them managed to appear under our tree, because to me – at least then – they seemed like gifts for a millionaire's child. Then the wonderful dinner, sometimes just us, often shared with other missionary families. Each year, as another Christmas day would come to an end, there was that special warmth of knowing that I was loved, pampered, had the best family ever and didn't have a care in the world.

One particular Christmas (I was nine) I had seen a beautiful doll in the window of a store that specialized in imported items. I knew I could never have her as she was too expensive, but I still loved standing at that window looking at her. My brother wanted a tricycle, and I definitely knew there would not be enough money for both of our dreams to come true. Yet – lo and behold – my dream doll and Gerry's trike were under the tree on Christmas morning! We were told how special ladies in the USA (United Foursquare Women) had sent the money for my parents to buy us Christmas presents...those ladies will never know the great joy they brought to us.

****

There were always weddings. I sang at them, was flower girl, junior bridesmaid, bridesmaid, maid of honor – you name it, I did it all at some point. At a much later point in life, I made wedding cakes, sewed for the brides, decorated the church, held receptions in our home and even performed a double wedding ceremony for two sisters in Argentina.

But the one wedding I remember the most actually started for me the day before the ceremony...I was probably around ten and had been out riding my bike which had just come home from the repair shop. I thought the best place to try it out would be on a steep, graveled hill at the edge of our neighborhood. Everything was going great as I sped down the hill with the wind blowing through my hair. It was fantastic! That is, until I looked ahead and saw my front wheel heading in a different direction than I was headed, then looked down to see the handlebars, unattached, gripped in my hands. I proceeded to lose my grip, literally and figuratively, and the next thing I knew I was rolling down the hill head over heels, trying to keep the gravel out of my face, finally landing with a thud at the front fence of a house at the bottom of the hill.

The noise brought the lady of the house running quickly to the door. She asked for my phone number and my dad came rushing to the scene. Although my pride was much more wounded than my body, I certainly did look a mess, with gravel embedded in my legs and arms and my face scratched and also gravel damaged. Daddy took me home to have Mommy clean and patch me up. Her first comment was, "Oh no, look at you! You have to be in a wedding tomorrow!" Well, it didn't take too terribly long to apply the necessary first aid, but it sure took a long time to powder the scratches on my face and arms the next afternoon so that I would "look half-way decent" for the wedding!

****

A definitive moment that will be forever engraved in my memory was on a particular morning when I walked by the small area designated as my father's study, and saw him sitting with his head bowed, tears streaming down his face. It panicked me, and I ran to get my mother as I was sure disaster was about to strike. When my mother came, I stood outside trying to listen, and when she asked him what was wrong, I heard him say he just felt like he wasn't doing enough to spread the Gospel in Honduras. Of course, that set my mother to crying as well, and soon I could hear them in intense prayer. I knew then that everything would be OK, because it always was when my parents prayed. I never stopped needing or relying on those prayers!

My world was filled with church meetings, open-air campaigns, watching my parents help people both spiritually, physically and financially, and the never-ending beginnings of new churches throughout the country. When I thought of people, I thought in terms of large groups; foreigners to me were people in other towns where we had not yet gone to hold meetings; entertainment was me – singing in the meetings; an exciting event to look forward to was going on a trip to a new town or village. I became the church pianist at around the age of thirteen and played until I left Honduras. I remember very few best friends as I grew up, but I certainly remember many best places to go and hold meetings.

I traveled a lot with my Daddy when I was not in school, interpreting for him and any USA visitors we might have along and, of course, singing in the services. I always loved traveling to a little town called Nacaome in Honduras. The village had no electricity and light was provided by flashlights and Coleman lamps. As the time for the service would draw near, you could see flashlights swinging in the dark as people walked – many of them several miles – to church. Then imagine with me four women, one standing in each corner of the church building, balancing a Coleman lamp on her head to light the service! I believe there were three sets of ladies that took turns, providing ample light for the service.

The first time I visited there, I spent more time watching this feat than paying attention to the service! I just knew one of those lamps would fall off and we would all have to scramble outside before the adobe, thatched-roof building burned down, but it never happened. I know that was a good thing, but always a little disappointing to me.

Then there was the fun of interpreting for guest speakers. Since I was the one to learn Spanish first, it was natural that I would do the interpreting for the simple Gospel messages preached. I loved doing this, but like any kid, after about the first 15 minutes I would start to lose interest and really had to discipline myself to concentrate and stay with the program. I soon learned this was really not intended to be fun but was a serious duty that I somehow needed to master. I don't know what other kids around the world were doing at eight, nine, ten years of age, but I have a feeling few were interpreting for adult preachers. And I have been interpreting ever since.

Children are quite creative when their social circle is small or limited; they conjure up an imaginary friend. I was no different, except that my imaginary friend was an imaginary people group (nation?). And I was their caretaker (missionary?). I had my own entire imagined little "nether land" under my bed, filled with very tiny people who had to be preached to, sang to, taught Sunday School lessons to, and in general be taken care of for clothing and food. I had my own mission organization that supplied all these needs, and I was the head of it, including maintaining financial records! OK…before you think I was weird or something, I was just a kid and it was more like a game; and I really thought through some great organizational skills that have served me throughout life. When one of my own daughters, Rebecca, acquired an imaginary friend, it did not worry me in the least, as I was quite confident she would outgrow it and learn some things along the way, just like I did.

****

In late 1957 we moved to a larger house that sat up on a hill, the river running down below us. There was a lot of political upheaval going on at that time, and one morning, after a night of hearing fighting quite close to the house (probably down along the riverbed) we found the remains of hand grenades outside our home. There continued to be scattered uprisings until 1958 when things calmed down with a duly elected president taking over the command, President Ramon Villeda Morales. For reasons I never understood, he was known as "Pajarito," or Little Bird.

When I was twelve, my family added a new member, my little sister, Judy. It began by my father taking large cans of powdered milk to a needy family on a weekly basis for the new baby in the home. Upon the illness of the grandmother who was raising her, he brought her home to be cared for until her family worked things out. Days turned into weeks, weeks into months, and we are still "caring" for her many years later! After having her in our home for several months, my mother suffered a miscarriage and there was no way we could give Judy up.

After much red tape and legal run-around, we were finally able to celebrate – she became Judith Kay Gurney and was ours for keeps. My first attempts at sewing were to make clothes for Judy. I have done a lot of sewing since then, what with four daughters, my own clothes, wedding dresses for young ladies that could not afford one, one of my own daughter's wedding dresses, dozens of bridesmaids dresses, prom dresses, wedding dress and prom dress alterations and remodeling for granddaughters and all sorts of crafts and articles for our home. Sewing is one of the arts that has fallen by the wayside but is so very useful. I don't think I would have survived without it.

Usually about once a year we would travel to a small town, San Marcos de Colón, close to the border of Nicaragua, to visit the Dymonds who were Assembly of God missionaries. They had a daughter my age, and Vicky and I loved getting into mischief together. One afternoon we decided to rent a couple of horses and ride to Nicaragua – just to say we had. We didn't tell our parents where we were going, only that we were going riding for a couple of hours. It was all good until we started back home and my horse suddenly sat down, my legs pinned under it, and refused to get up. After what seemed like forever a couple of farmers came along and got the horse up, but it refused to move with me on it. So, I climbed up behind Vicky and held on to the reins for the horse to follow us. We finally made it home, albeit a little later than planned, and discovered the next morning when we went to rent horses again, that the horse I had been riding had a new colt! Poor girl, I felt really bad, but it was just another adventure Vicky and I shared.

We moved again early 1959, and, again, we were close to the river which we would ford to leave our neighborhood as the bridge had been washed out. My knowledge of anatomy grew at that time, as we would ford the river while (naked) men and (half nude) women would be bathing as we drove by. Not long after we moved into that house, I fell down the flight of fourteen tiled concrete stairs, from top to bottom, hitting my tail bone on every step. No doubt that is where my back issues stem from that I have dealt with most of my adult life.

It was while we were living there that we witnessed more political unrest, with fighting going on very near our home. A family from the church that we were close to lived across the river, even nearer to the fighting than we were, and brought what groceries they had and stayed with us for a couple of days.

****

Being closely involved in the mission work, I came to understand at an early age that being a missionary is not an easy thing. My brother decided when he was quite young that being a missionary was a great career – especially if you were in the USA on furlough! (He later changed his mind – packing was the first thing that put him off.) On our first furlough I was eleven and Gerry was three. His English was limited; he understood quite well but refused to speak it, so his adaptation to live with my grandparents most of that year while our parents itinerized was at times strained. He was so excited to see his first snow and ran outside barefoot in his undies to play in the white mud. He quickly ran inside crying that he didn't like that cold white mud!

But furloughs are short-lived and the daily truth of being far away from grandparents, aunts, uncles and cousins was often quite daunting. As I approached my teen years, I began to question whether I wanted to be a missionary myself. Not that I ever intended leaving Honduras, and I gave much thought to what I could do there as a career – teach English, be a sales person, work at the American Embassy – a lot of possibilities crossed my young mind.

I was not overly interested in what God had in mind for me if it meant having to leave Honduras.

Right around my fourteenth birthday, I woke up in the middle of the night very sick. My parents rushed me to the highest recommended hospital in Tegucigalpa and it was soon determined that I had severe appendicitis. The best surgeon was called in and I went into surgery. The incision was much longer than normal, and my recuperation took a long time. It wasn't long after my surgery that my parents discovered that the "best surgeon," as it turned out, was also an alcoholic. Many years and four pregnancies later I had to have some reconstructive surgery, at which time it was discovered that I had never been properly sewn up inside and had some five pounds of adhesions removed. During that fourteenth year of my life I also served as first grade teacher to my brother, using the Calvert correspondence method.

· V ·

Teenage Turmoils

*"Happiness comes through doors you
didn't even know were open."*

While most US girls my age were doing sports, trying out for cheerleading, experimenting with make-up and
fashion, going to parties and proms and, in general, doing
all the fun things US teenagers do, I was getting up at 5:30
each morning, having breakfast (which Daddy made and
insisted I eat) then going to emcee a half hour radio program from 6:30 to 7:00 am. I headed from there to a bilingual secretarial school for the rest of the morning; then
home for lunch and an afternoon of high school studies by
correspondence through the University of Nebraska, followed by Bible Institute at night. In retrospect, I may have
been over-doing it a bit and over-compensating in other
areas that I considered my "fun" time; but I survived and
learned some hard lessons along the way. The radio program I started at the age of fourteen still continues today.
When I visited Honduras in 2002, I was awakened my first
morning there by the sound of my younger self singing the

program's theme song. "Wonderful Words of Life," that I had recorded many years before!

Shortly before my fifteenth birthday I had my first job, working during the school break at the Baptist Book Store run by the Baptist missionary Harold Hurst, whose family we had been very close to since shortly after our arrival in Honduras.

Around this same time I met Ramon and Ruben Morales, the teenaged twin sons of the president of Honduras. They had a red (imported) convertible sports car, probably the only one in the country, and came by one afternoon offering to take me for a ride. You don't say no to that – at least I didn't! My parents were out of town, so I told the maid/nanny I was going off for a ride. After about a half hour I kept feeling like we were being followed and asked the guys about it. They laughed and told me it was just their personal guards that followed them everywhere for protection, not to worry because they were well armed and would take down anyone that tried to harm us. Although I enjoyed the fun, I was a bit scared off and turned them down the next time they stopped by. My parents were not too happy about it when I told them after they returned from their trip.

My fifteenth birthday was joyfully celebrated by a surprise party the youth group planned, followed by a serenade at midnight by a group of the guys. Shortly after my birthday, I came to the States to spend a summer with my grandparents in Woodburn. I had a wonderful summer, went on some real dates for the first time (double dates, some of them with my Aunt Rosella and Uncle Wayne!), learned how to bowl and attended summer church camp. I guess the thrill of the lifestyle helped my rebellion set in, and I decided I would NEVER be a missionary.

However, God had other plans. While attending summer camp, the guest speaker (Dr. Charles W. Walkem) asked me to sing at the close of one of the services. He asked that I sing the old hymn, "I'll Go Where You Want Me to Go." While singing, I broke down and said yes to God's call to missions, but I was still not fully convinced.

Back in Honduras, it was Christmas 1960 that I finally was granted permission by my parents to go with the youth group caroling from house to house, eating along the way, and having a ton of fun. I had begged for the last couple of years to do so and was so excited I finally could go. Following the Christmas Eve program, in which I was an angel, I hurried home with my parents to change and be ready when the youth group came by...only to look in the mirror and notice how swollen my cheeks were. Yep, I had the mumps. So much for caroling. Déjà vu – my horse-back ride with Gary back on the Oregon farm. Not going to happen!

Upon my return to Honduras after the summer months spent in the USA, I know I was a trial to my parents during the following months. My forms of seeking attention for what I wanted to do took some bizarre twists, including a much older boyfriend. It was decided early in 1961 that the best thing for me would be to leave Honduras and have a North American high school experience. My parents told the Missions Board they needed to find a home for me or they would return from the field. Rev. Leita Mae Steward, long-time secretary to Dr. Rolf K. McPherson, president of the Foursquare denomination, suggested I go to live with her sister and family, Roberta and Glenn Harris. (Oddly enough, Glenn and Roberta were Steve Harris' aunt and uncle.) I was soon preparing to travel.

The departure from Honduras was extremely difficult for me, far more than I could have anticipated. Leaving the country, life, childhood memories, church, friends, first "love," and, most of all, my family, was far more traumatic than I had imagined. Add to that the fact that I had never met the family I was to live with – neither had my parents, for that matter – and you can perhaps sympathize with the outgoing, independent girl that suddenly had qualms about what was ahead in some little town called Victorville, California. My mother called the Mission's Director to request permission for her to travel with me to the States, as she would not send me alone; if I was to go, she would go with me, to meet the family herself and be assured that I would be taken care of.

It was at this time in my life when I decided I wouldn't dwell on the good-byes for too long…rather, I would enjoy the eternal hellos and savor each and every person who came into my life. My Honduran friends have been a part of my entire life. Many of them have passed on and many have moved to different parts of the world. I remain good friends with my first boyfriend, Israel, and his family, and he has spent his life serving the Lord, and a great many others have continued to be friends as well.

I could never have imagined the life-long impact that move was to have on my life. As a teenage missionary kid who had lived out of the US for most of my life and needed to finish high school, it would take some time for me to realize that the home and love Glenn and Roberta Harris offered me were unbelievable gifts of destiny. My life was touched and marked forever.

Arriving at their home on a windy, sand-blasted

winter day in early February 1961, my mother and I walked into the pleasant atmosphere of a small house in what seemed to be the middle of nowhere in the desert, and certainly, in my eyes, the end of the earth. But I was quickly drawn by the main piece of furniture in the front room, a piano. As their daughter Marilyn and I were introduced, we instinctively moved toward that piano, sat down on the bench, and began to play and sing together. My mother says that it was at that moment when she knew it would all be OK. I cannot imagine how difficult it had to be for her to take me there, leave me after only a very few days in my new atmosphere, and return to Honduras without me. I do know how hard it was for me to watch her leave.

Little did I know that the months I would spend in Victorville would determine the entire rest of my life. It was there I would come face to face with making permanent, life-long decisions and meet people that would become an integral part of me forever. In great part, my life is what it is today due to the time spent in that home – I met my husband there (both of them, actually!), acquired two more "sisters" and a new "brother"; and eventually, out of that family, a much loved son-in-law and then three precious grandchildren, great grandchildren, not to mention the many nieces and nephews I proudly claim including Sherri, David, Debbie and Don and their children. I can now proudly claim Don as my son-in-love, and a granddaughter-in-love, Katelyn (Debbie's daughter) who married my grandson, Justin (Brenda's son) and two great grandsons...so far.

Only God can put something like that together, through a life yielded to Him! What then seemed like an inconvenient space of time to me, was actually God's definitive time of life-long preparation. *"Lord, you have assigned me my portion and my cup; you have made my lot secure. The boundary lines for me have fallen in pleasant places; surely I have a delightful inheritance. Therefore, my heart is glad and my tongue rejoices."* Psalm 16:5-6.

****

Marilyn and I had so much fun together. At one point, we kept trying to wake up earlier each morning to figure out at what time the sprinklers would come on at the park one-half block away. When we finally figured it out, we went down and started swinging just before they would come on so we could get soaked by surprise...of course we had to keep quiet and couldn't yell out when the cold water hit us, as the rest of the neighborhood was still sleeping. And we loved sleeping on the flat roof-top of the house; however, we were a little surprised when we awoke one morning to find our sleeping bags covered in snow!

Then there's the time we went to sing on a Friday night at the little Foursquare Church in Barstow. We had formed a trio, "The Melodettes", together with her cousin, Margie. It was all great until we headed for home, Marilyn at the wheel because she "knew the way." About a half hour into our trip we were suddenly stopped by armed, uniformed men...We had driven out onto the firing range of the nearby Marine base!

One Saturday we had driven down to San Bernardino, the "in" place to shop, to look for school clothes. We weren't having a lot of luck with our shopping, and getting a little bored, decided to go up to some older lady, a complete stranger, and tell her how great it was to see her again.

(I claim ownership of this brilliant idea.) We did, and of course she was confused, and we told her how excited our mom would be to know we had seen her. She responded with an invitation for us to come out to visit the doll factory...She owned the Terry Lee Doll Factory that operated on the high desert!

We saved our coins for gas and treats in a mason jar in the glove compartment of the little '42 Ford Marilyn drove. On any given Friday night (if we didn't have a date), our favorite thing to do was to cruise over to the A&W, have an ice cold root beer or a float, and check out who might be hanging out there. Or, if you happened to be downtown Victorville in the middle of the summer of 1961, you may have heard a couple of crazy girls driving around (me driving Jerry's car!) singing Christmas carols at the top of our lungs. Those were great days!

I truly enjoyed the church in Victorville, and loved the pastors, Paul and Ruth Smith. They were young, enthusiastic, and she was drop-dead gorgeous to boot. (Mike named Rebecca and gave her the middle name of Ruth because he too thought she was drop-dead gorgeous and loved her dimples!) I baby-sat for them from time to time and became quite attached to the family. The church youth group was fun, I became involved in Sunday School, and of course, sang in church often. During those very first weeks, a group of young people from L.I.F.E. Bible College came to have a Sunday night service, and I was introduced to a young student named Michael Frederick, a tall, dark, handsome twenty-year old – I was a mere fifteen; he did not remember the occasion, so we'll talk about that later. On that same evening I met two other L.I.F.E. students, Steve and Nancy Harris.

According to the credits I had earned through my high school studies by correspondence, I was in the middle of my junior year when Roberta took me to enroll at Victor Valley Senior High School. The classes I still needed were not difficult; I threw in Spanish as a no-brainer elective, and Speech as a challenge. I was right on both counts – I never cracked a book in Spanish class and became a state-wide contender in the Speech Contests sponsored by the Lion's Club. I also acquired a bit of popularity by my singing in school events and even did a few gigs at George Air Force Base, with Marilyn playing for me.

During the summer between my junior and senior years, I needed to take a couple of summer school courses as I'd never had US History, much less California History. I enjoyed them both and met a couple of the funniest guys I have ever known, who remained among my close friends during my senior year. It was during those months that I was approached by a talent scout from Los Angeles to do a demo for a recording company, but felt I had to turn down the opportunity due to the attitude towards the entertainment field that prevailed in the church world at that time.

The only subject that gave me some pause was math; I was placed in an algebra class. Due to my father's early math training that math should be useful, I totally detested algebra and after a week of it sought out my school counselor for another possible option. He placed me in Business Math and I loved it and excelled – it had a purpose! I graduated from high school one month after my seventeenth birthday, was named to "Who's Who Among High School Students of America" and picked up a few scholarships along the way.

During my first summer in Victorville and through my senior year, I mainly dated a young man who graduated a year ahead of me and went to Biola College. I dated a few others along the way, but Jerry was my main guy. As I came close to graduation, I began to realize that our spiritual roads did not seem to merge, and although I was hesitant to break up with him, I knew it was something that would need to be dealt with soon.

So it was that on May 5, 1962 (my seventeenth birthday), I was attending a huge all-day picnic celebration for the golden anniversary of the senior Harrises (Glenn's parents) and I was again introduced to Michael Frederick... This time he noticed and never forgot it! It was love at second sight for me – I had already met him, and it was only a very short time before I knew he was Mr. Right. He vows and declares he also knew it upon meeting me...the second time, that is! It became quite clear that I would have to deal with Jerry soon.

As fate (or Roberta's sense of humor) would have it, she had invited Jerry to have dinner with us on a Saturday evening just shortly after I met Mike. Jerry accepted, then called and told me he couldn't make it. Since Mike was in town for the weekend from college, Roberta asked me if I would like to invite him to dinner instead. Of course I did, and of course he said yes, regardless of what previous plans he may have had! Between Mike's acceptance of the dinner date, sometime around 3:30 p.m., and dinner time, 6:00 p.m., Jerry called back and told Roberta he would indeed be able to make it after all. She told him to come right on.

Well, she never shared this little tidbit of information with me, so come dinner time I found myself sitting between the two of them. Talk about the makings for indigestion! I could tell Mike was seething so in an attempt to assuage his mood, I leaned my knee against his to let him know he was the one I was really with. He turned and looked at me and said, in a low, ornery voice, "Where's the other one?"

I guess Jerry was on edge as well, because after dinner he asked me to go out on the porch for a talk. I don't remember a great deal of the conversation, only that he said he realized the conflict between my Pentecostal roots and his non-Pentecostal perspective would have to be dealt with. I am not sure what he expected, but the decision was double easy for me, what with my Pentecostal roots running deep and Mike sitting a few feet away behind a closed door. When I told Jerry my decision, he got in his car, laid rubber for about a block, and I never saw him again.

It was only many years later that we enjoyed a friendly phone conversation, catching each other up on what life had been for us, followed by a delightful visit Steve and I recently had with him. I do respect him and his faithfulness to the Lord and will be forever grateful to him for helping me through the difficult months in the strange place I found myself upon returning from Honduras. He was a wonderful Christian guy, lots of fun and had a great deal of patience with the odd fate dealt him in the form of a missionary kid for a girlfriend!

****

The outstanding facts of my graduation were the all-night at Disneyland party we bussed to as a class. I went with a friend one class behind me, (as Jerry and I were no longer an item and Mike had college that night!) and we had a blast. Nothing like eating breakfast at 4:00 a.m. at Disneyland! Then, it was so windy the evening of graduation that we had to hold our caps on our heads as we bravely marched onto the wind-swept football field. We had a major emergency as we debated which hand we should use for that purpose so we would all look the same...I think we opted for our left hand as we would be using the right hand to move our tassels.

Immediately following graduation, a group of ten of us from the church, with our pastor Paul Smith, took a mission trip to Monterrey, Mexico. We all rode in a camper shell and took turns riding two at a time in the cab with the pastor. We stopped and held a couple of services on our way to help finance our trip. I was going to translate and a young man from Honduras who was at L.I.F.E. also was to translate. Following our service in El Paso, Texas, we had yet another young man who insisted on going along, and our pastor approved. The only problem was that our new recruit had an ulterior motive – me! It took a few disconcerting days to convince him I wasn't interested.

Returning stateside from that trip, we understood we had to be out of Mexico by a certain time (late at night) that coincided with our entry date. We were all asleep in the camper when I was awakened by hearing our pastor say in a very strong, loud voice, "Usted es estúpido!" I realized we had a major problem and jumping out of the camper I proceeded to calm everyone down, explained the confusion about the date of our departure and beg forgiveness for our pastor's lack of Spanish and his concern due to being responsible for all of us. Just as I got it all settled and we were about to take off, our Honduran member stuck his head out the window of the camper to find out was going on! Of course, now the border guards thought we were smuggling someone out of Mexico. Some 30 minutes and much explaining later, we were finally on our way.

Still holding to the decision that I did not want to be a missionary, but at the same time realizing I needed to listen to God, I had come to what I believed to be a most wise conclusion: I didn't mind marrying a pastor or such, but not a missionary. That was simple – I just wouldn't date missionary material! Voilà – what was hard about that? And believe me, Mike was not your obvious missionary candidate. With his hot car, he was known to hit the drag strip instead of church on many given Sundays, held the record at the Fontana race track for quite a lengthy time, had a reputation for girls falling hard for him when he was totally uninterested and spent a pretty hefty sum of his income on the latest clothes. Pastor? Maybe. Missionary? Never! I was on safe ground.

Two months after we met, my parents were on furlough and relaxing in a desert cabin when Mike visited them and asked them for my hand in marriage. They were stunned, did not know him (in fact when they arrived in the USA they thought I was still dating blonde Jerry and wondered who in the world the dark-haired young man was that I showed up with at the airport), and thought it was all pretty sudden! But Mike prevailed, and the next day we sat in the little park just a block from the Harris home. It was there he proposed to me. His proposal did not take me by surprise. His words did!

"Lolita, I know you have a call to missions as I do, and I believe God has brought us together to spend our lives together serving Him." Whoa! Say WHAT? Oh dear…I guess the old adage that he who laughs last, laughs best, is indeed true; and God certainly got the last laugh on that one! He must be still laughing about it, all these many years later!

One of the advantages of being bilingual and not looking the part is that you have an automatic shock factor ability. Like the Saturday Mike took me to a great amusement park that used to be down on the beach in Santa Monica called, "Pacific Ocean Park," known as POP. It was one of our favorite fun spots and we always had a fantastic time there. On this particular day, while standing in line waiting to get on a ride, a couple of Hispanic guys fell into line behind us. They immediately began to talk about me, pretty much verbally undressing me, in Spanish of course. I listened for a couple of minutes, had about as much of it as I could take, then turned around and in my perfect Spanish said, "Either you better shut up or I'll tell my boyfriend here what you were saying!" Mike was about twice as tall as them. Their mouths literally fell open, they turned around and walked quickly away. Great fun!

From possibly Biola or Pepperdine for college, due to scholarships, I found my way to L.I.F.E. Bible College in September of 1962, had an engagement ring on my hand by Thanksgiving Day, and plans began for a June 22, 1963 wedding. We were married in Angelus Auditorium next door to where my parents had been married, and Pastor Paul Smith and the then Mission's Director of our organization, Dr. Herman Mitzner, tied the knot. I wore my mother's wedding gown which had been altered by my friend Lilia Soto, who also made the bridesmaids dresses. I insisted my father would only be my Daddy on that day, give me away and sing the Lord's prayer. My parents looked so beautiful to me, and I was very proud to be their daughter as I became Mike's wife. On that day I realized that missions or no missions, Mike was forever.

· VI ·

Getting My Missionary Feet Wet – Again

"Making a 'living' is not the same thing as making a 'life'."

My Great Aunt Lela used to have a saying, "Needles and pins, needles and pins; when you get married your trouble begins." I never understood why she thought that was such a good saying, but I was embarking on the road to find out! Our married life began in a little apartment two blocks off Sunset Boulevard in Los Angeles, with Mike getting up at the crack of dawn to go work a long, hard day at a factory some forty minutes away and me getting up about an hour later to work all day at a doctor's office. We would reunite around 5:15 each evening, have a quick dinner, then be off to classes, followed by homework, reading, bedtime, and start all over again the next day. Our weekends were composed of taking our dirty clothes to Mike's parents' home, Cleo and Fannie Frederick, in Bloomington. I would launder the clothes and hang them on the lines. Then we would head on to Victorville for the rest of the weekend, where Mike was now assistant pastor. On our way home after church on Sunday night, we would stop by his folks to pick up the folded clothes – thanks to my mother-in-law – and back home for another long week of work and studies. Whew!

Mike graduated from L.I.F.E. Bible College in February 1964 and we immediately left on a Missionary Assist program, sponsored by the Harris Transportation Company under the auspices of the Victorville Foursquare Church, heading to San Pedro Sula, Honduras. As we prepared to leave, it amazed us how things fell into place – we were able to sell what few large items we had, including our car; and as expenses would come up for the trip, the exact amount needed to cover the expenses came in from unexpected places. For me, the excitement of "going home" was great, but this would be Mike's first experience of living outside the USA – with no knowledge of Spanish.

Mike was twenty-three and a half, I was three months shy of turning nineteen. We would be filling in for a single missionary lady, Mattie Sensabaugh, who was going on furlough. Oh yes – and we even had a real salary…$150 a month, with a mission house provided. But then, when you are young and in love, who needs money? San Pedro Sula was a hot, humid, rainy, steamy city, second only to the weather that must have existed in the pressure cooker I used for cooking beans on an almost daily basis. The upside was that we were a mere one very long day's trip from my family in Tegucigalpa.

Regarding that house I mentioned, it sat behind the church, facing the side street. It was obviously handy to be on site, as we had only public transportation; however, the congregation had previously had free come-and-go privileges of the house as well as of the church. The first time I was walking across the hall from our bedroom to the bathroom in my slip, in full view of a young man relaxing in our front room, we had a problem – Mike had a big problem. We proceeded to acquire a little dog that very quickly grew into a big barking maniac, particularly if anyone stepped out the back door of the church. Everyone knew his ferocious bark. What we didn't reveal was that he had no bite – he wouldn't hurt a flea. So the home-invasion problem was soon corrected.

The second undesirable feature of the house was the tenants living in the rafters. These were good sized iguanas that could be seen periodically sunning themselves on our protective, glass embedded, property wall, and heard consistently by us in the house. I lived in fear that one of those thumping monsters would fall through the ceiling and land on our dining room table, in the middle of the kitchen or – God forbid – on our bed. Despite our best efforts to smoke them out, scare them out, lure them out with bait for a possible kill, they remained in their living quarters the entire time we were there...but never came through the ceiling, for which I am eternally grateful!

While in San Pedro Sula we became very involved with an orphanage that was run by Berniece Fogelberg, who had graduated from L.I.F.E. Bible College many years earlier. I had known her since my childhood years in Honduras and had been friends with her daughter, Juanita, before we both went stateside. Berniece was a real encouragement to us. We shared many humble meals, birthday parties and night-watches over sick children with her. It was after a day of playing with the boys in a mango orchard that Mike discovered he had a very severe allergy to mangos!

(Incidentally, so did my mother.) Mike also had the unique privilege of dedicating tiny triplet baby girls to the Lord that had been left at the orphanage. I still look back on the beautiful memories of watching all the children walk into our church for Sunday School on Sunday mornings. One of the little boys became Mike's shadow; he is now a pastor here in the US who would hug on Mike whenever our paths crossed and thank him for loving him when he was a little orphan in Honduras. That, my friends, is what makes it all worthwhile!

We celebrated our first anniversary by going to a recently opened little restaurant we had heard about, a pizza parlor, which was, in itself, a rarity in Honduras. We had saved up for our big splurge, and when we were seated and began looking around the small restaurant, we thought it strange that the walls of an Italian pizzeria were decorated with souvenirs from Argentina. There was a large map of the country just above our table, a travel poster proclaiming the wonders of the city of Buenos Aires on the opposite wall, and numerous pictures of gauchos and tango dancers scattered in various places. We had no idea that Argentina had a high ratio of Italians among its population, but while we were sitting there eating our pizza, a very strange thing happened. We looked at each other, and almost simultaneously said, "We will be there some day." Was that a decision, a prophetic word, an epiphany…or all of the above? Call it what you will, it determined our destiny.

The morning after our anniversary dinner, Mike awoke with a stomach virus; later that morning we received a telegram telling us of the passing of Mike's dad the day before (on our anniversary). It "so happened" that Glenn and Roberta Harris arrived for a visit on that same day and made it possible for Mike to fly home for the funeral. Marilyn stayed on with us in Honduras for a couple of months.

Some of the most difficult times of our lives took place in San Pedro Sula. Shortly after our first Christmas there, I suffered a miscarriage and we were both heartbroken. Berniece helped me with the medical aspects of the event, and my parents came over as soon as they heard to take care of the emotional aspects.

Just a very few weeks after I had lost our baby, I answered the door and was faced with a young couple who attended our church when they came to the city from their village. In her arms the mother held a baby, which she handed to me. Her husband said, "Our baby was just pronounced dead. We want you to prepare him for burial and then want your husband to have the funeral." At nineteen, I was totally unprepared for anything like that, but knew that they had twenty-four hours in which to take care of the burial and did not have the heart to argue with them.

We sent out word through the associate pastors that lived close by that there would be a funeral that afternoon, and I searched out something appropriate in which to dress the baby from the mission barrel of supplies I kept on hand. While I dressed the already cold child, Mike prepared a funeral service. At the end of the day, I had never felt so exhausted and drained; but there was a deep sense of reward for having walked through the valley of death with them and somehow been a help along the way.

Not many weeks later we went to minister in the village of La Union where we had to travel by bus and then by horseback. The entire village had been won to Christ, and Bible teaching was in great demand. We stayed in the home of the wealthiest landowner in the area and were treated like royalty. In the mornings I taught some much-needed classes to train the brand-new Sunday school teachers, and Mike preached in the evening services while I interpreted. The first night, just as he got up to preach, a young girl (probably about fourteen) started to become agitated and disrupt the service. They finally got her calmed down and the sermon continued. The second night the same thing happened; on the third night we recognized it was the enemy trying to distract from the preaching of the Word. Mike went over to her and began to rebuke the enemy, and in a very gruff voice, the girl responded to him in perfect English! (When we asked later, we learned she knew absolutely no English and had never even heard it spoken!) We had her taken out of the building and continued to deal with her until the demonic powers finally were loosed. Her entire facial look and demeanor completely changed, and she was free from then on.

Oh yes…it seems that it was while we were in La Union that we placed our order for another baby, which resulted in the birth of our precious first daughter. God was good to us.

A frustrating situation we faced was when a "big-time US evangelist" came to preach at the church. He came well recommended (no doubt because the person recommending him was anxious to get rid of him), and, unfortunately, we were gullible and believed the recommendation! He was to stay with us for a couple of days, preach one night, then leave. As he did not speak Spanish, I had to interpret for him, which was really a very good thing, because I ended up preaching a totally different sermon than he did, due to some theologically off-the-wall statements he was expounding...which was also a very bad thing, because I preached a pretty good sermon that night and the people were blessed and thrilled. So, our guest decided that since he had been such a blessing, he would stay a couple of more nights! We tried to persuade him to leave, but rather than enter into a heated argument, we decided to go ahead and let him stay, and I simply re-preached the same sermon the second and third night and people began to stay home.

We were relieved, thinking that he would now leave. But after feeding him for another two days, he brought home a young street boy – unknown to him – to live in our house as well! This was not something smart, as the street boys were known to get people to feel sorry for them, let them in their house to eat and maybe sleep for a night, and they were then used by the underworld to let in thieves or even murderers, once they were inside a home. It was the first and one of the few times I ever saw my husband REALLY mad, and he set his foot down. The "evangelist" then confessed that his US passport had expired and he had no place to go – so we graciously called the American Consulate for him, reported him, and they came and took care of the rest. We were extremely grateful, for not only had our patience run out, but so had our food supply.

The first months of marriage are wonderful, and a young couple does want to spend all the time possible together. However, spending 24/7 with me and not being able to talk to anyone unless I was there to interpret for him, must have been extremely frustrating for my young, formerly independent, husband. So it was that one hot, steamy afternoon Mike informed me he was going to walk to town to purchase a few personal items. I asked if he would like me to go along, and he emphatically said, "No, I want to go by myself."

I wondered how he would manage and was curious as to what he would come back with. When he arrived home, he showed me his purchases: toothpaste, deodorant and soap. I asked him how he had managed, and he told me he had simply said, "Quiero para (I want for)...." and made a motion to brush his teeth, "Quiero para... "and made a show of applying deodorant, and, "Quiero para...." while imitating the action of rubbing soap on under a shower. I was most relieved that we didn't need toilet paper! He also asked me what "Qué guapo" meant; I was a bit ticked to learn that some young chick had told him he was handsome!

The last big adventure of our one and a half years tour of duty in Honduras took place a very short time after I realized I was again pregnant. My parents had invited us to go with them to San Salvador, El Salvador, for a few days' holiday. We were really excited, as it would be our first vacation since our honeymoon. We traveled over to Tegucigalpa and from there to El Salvador with my parents. They had reserved rooms for us at a bed and breakfast type home owned by an American lady, and it was indeed very pleasant, built in the typical colonial style, around a large indoor courtyard. The courtyard had beautiful, huge clay pots filled with flowering tropical plants, the rooms were small but clean and comfortable with narrow twin beds, and the food on the evening we arrived was wonderful.

Being exhausted from the trip, we all retired early, only to be brusquely awakened in the wee hours of the morning by an extremely strong earthquake. Mike and I jumped out of our beds and headed for the door jam, the best place for protection. All the lights had gone out. I had on a respectable nightgown, and seeing a light in the hallway, I grabbed the candle from the side of my bed and went to see if I could get it lit. I approached the bearer of light and asked him if he would mind lighting my candle from his. As he reached out to do so, he suddenly looked down and said, "Oh – sorry, I can't; I don't have any clothes on," and walked off! Like I cared?

We went out to the courtyard as another wave of shudders rolled through the streets and building. Those giant clay pots were rolling around like small basketballs. Across the street was a Catholic church, and people began streaming to it to pray for protection. When the movements finally died down, we all went back to bed. I was still pretty frightened and got into that very narrow little twin bed with my husband, which turned out to be a wise choice, as shortly after, a good size chunk of wall fell on the bed where I had been sleeping. As the sun came up, we packed up what little we had brought with us, jumped in the car and headed back to Honduras. On our way, we passed through some small villages that were completely leveled by the earthquake. The vacation was not the easy-going restful interlude we had anticipated, but certainly was memorable.

****

In late June of 1965 we returned to the States, via a short stop in Mexico City for a two-day vacation. We arrived back in Victorville, California, in the heat of the desert summer, I was pregnant, no car and ready to start over from scratch. At that time, our Mission Board had a stipulation that before an applicant could be appointed as a missionary, two years of state-side pastoral experience was required. In our case, the Mission Board had offered to make an exception and send us as missionaries as soon as we returned, counting Mike's experience as assistant pastor in Victorville and our experience in San Pedro Sula as sufficient. However, at some point during our engagement, someone had made the comment to Mike that, "one sure way of making it to the mission field was by marrying a missionary's daughter." That did not please him in the least, and he was determined no exceptions would be made for us, so we sought a pastorate. But before leaving the Los Angeles area to take a pastoral position, we filled out the necessary missionary application forms, and in the space marked "Field of Calling," we put, "Latin America, preferably South America."

We were ultimately asked to take the pastorate of the Foursquare church in Bremerton, Washington, so we packed all our earthly belongings in the little white Comet we had purchased from Melvin Harris (my Victorville "brother") and headed across the desert and north to Washington. The vehicle had no air conditioning...this in the month of August; so we began our journey late one evening and carried a large thermos of water and towels that we kept wet and wrapped across our shoulders and around our necks in an effort to keep cool. We also had a box of sandwiches and cookies to nourish us during our travels.

The Bremerton church had some major challenges, mainly financial, but there were possibilities for growth.

There was a not quite completed walk-in basement, with plans to build the sanctuary on top. The parsonage was a small two bedroom home a short distance from the church that had housed the previous pastor, his wife and four boys...it needed some repairs and a face lift. Also, the oil bill at the house (for heating) had not been paid since the previous winter and needed to be taken care of before cool weather set in.

Fortunately, Bremerton was only four hours from both sets of my grandparents, aunts, uncles and cousins in Oregon. After a short visit to Oregon, where we were showered with some items we were in much need of for setting up housekeeping, we found ourselves as official pastors on the first Sunday in September of 1965. Mike took up school bus driving and I began settling us into the little parsonage in preparation for the arrival of our first child. My craving while pregnant was oatmeal...a good thing, since it was cheap! The salary we were paid ($25.00 a week) we gave back to the church to help pay off some debts, so money was scarce, but ingenuity was abundant. My relatives constantly brought us home-canned fruit, vegetables and salmon and the congregation also shared their bounty with us. We soon felt at home, and on November 23, 1965, welcomed Brenda Michelle into our hearts and home. What a day that was! She filled us with such love and joy – and has every day since.

We would take occasional ferry rides across Puget Sound to Seattle for an outing, visit pastors in the little town of Shelton, and make a trip about every four months to visit family in Oregon. For the most part, we stayed close to home in Bremerton, which had (at that time) the largest dry-dock in the USA, and we would get Navy families in the church for a few weeks and then they would all move again. It was hard to make friends, the weather was often damp and dreary, but we were happy in our little house with our new baby and a growing church.

We went to the International Foursquare Convention in February 1966 in Los Angeles, California; at that convention Brenda was dedicated by Dr. Herman Mitzner, Mission's director, Mike was ordained and I was licensed. In February 1967 we again traveled to the International Convention in Los Angeles. We had planned on driving our car and stopped in Woodburn to pick up my grandma who had offered to go with us and help with Brenda. Upon leaving Woodburn the next morning, we made it only about ten miles out of town when our car starting coughing and spewing. Grandma had a quick solution: go back to Woodburn, leave our car with a relative who was a mechanic, and drive her nearly new Rambler to California. Sounded like a great idea to us. If you ever heard the fifties song about the little Nash Rambler, I do believe it was written about Grandma's car with her behind the wheel! The little old lady from Pasadena had nothing over my Grandma McCarthy when it came to speeding!

During that convention we were appointed as missionaries! Déjà vu – February 1952! Our appointment would become effective September 1st of that year, two years to the Sunday since we had become the pastors in Bremerton. During that two-year period, we had all the church debts paid off, a new sanctuary built and dedicated and a parsonage that was fixed up as good as it could be. We considered our time there a success and could hardly believe we would soon be on our way to fulfill the Lord's call on our lives.

· VII ·

What Call?

*"Opportunities are never lost; if you don't
take them, someone else will."*

I want to take a little detour here from my story to
talk a bit about what is commonly referred to as "a call."
How often that term is used – and misused! Over the years
I have watched people fumble through what they thought
was a call, fight against what they knew was a call, some
turn their backs on their call, and others who were abun-
dantly blessed in so many ways for following their call.
The key question becomes, "What constitutes a call?" From
there it is a personal choice as to whether or not you obey
the call.

I am not talking about some mystical, audible
voice or a sudden spellbinding vision; those are very few
and light years between. I am talking about you and me,
everyday people, for whom God has a special plan and has
designed us to fulfill a special need in His kingdom. It may
be in full-time ministry, but it may very well also be in the
business or education world, medical field, entertainment

realm, politics, city employee, or any other venue where He may choose to place us. God's possibilities for serving Him are far greater than the span of our imagination – but He does have a place where He needs each of us individually.

I am a people watcher…short term (in airports!) as well as long term (life-long!). It is amazing how much we can learn from the histories of individuals. Watching people live out their lives and gleaning from their experiences is the highest form of education. My own life's road has placed me in a position to do this extensively. Over many years of being a spectator of the lives of others, I think I have learned some important facts about what a call is. Please allow me to share some thoughts with you.

1) First and foremost, we must DISCOVER and recognize there is need. How worthless it would be for me to decide to dedicate my life to inventing a paper clip! We already have an abundance of paper clips in every style, color and material imaginable. The world can only use so many types of paper clips. There is no requirement for more; that is not a need. However, when Dr. Vinton Johnson and Dr. Dick Scott began their ministry among the San Blas Indians of Panamá in the late fifties and sixties, it became immediately evident that there was a need for the translation of the Scriptures into that dialect. They recognized that need.

Missionaries throughout the ages have recognized the need for the spreading of the Gospel in remote outposts of the world, while others have seen the need in the inner cities and more civilized areas. Young graduates have seen a need for new types of computer programming over the last decades; medical science is presented daily with new forms of illnesses which demand the need for cures; farmers over the years have seen the need for better and faster equipment and new methods to supply the demand for food; teachers are constantly seeing the need for new methods of imparting knowledge; entrepreneurs envision the need for new systems and marketing plans on a daily basis; athletes are compelled to use their strengths to win for their team; pastors, missionaries and ministries of all types are faced daily with the needs of people trying to survive and succeed in an ever-changing world environment. The needs are great – the fields are white unto harvest in so many arenas. If your heart, mind and eyes are open, you will see the need.

The enemy of our souls would try to blind us to the needs, because he knows that *"where there is no vision, the people perish."* Proverbs 29:18. Our constant prayer should be that the Lord would open our eyes, both physical and spiritual, so that we can be aware and sensitive to the needy world around us.

2) The next step for the call is to know you have the abilities and DESIRE to assist in fulfilling the need…I truly believe God gives us the wisdom and ability to see where we are needed. You see the need and you get excited, thinking, "I can do something about that!" You realize God has given you some unique abilities and talents that can be used in a specific field of service. You may get excited and begin to think about how your abilities could be used. Your mind constantly goes back to the same thoughts…this is needed – I can do it! Help is required – I can help! Volunteers are being recruited – I can be one! It is thrilling to watch a person who has caught a vision and begins to dedicate themselves to its fulfillment.

Think about it: you have no doubt experienced that fired-up anticipation in your own life at some point or another as you ran after the quest of accomplishing something you knew you had the capabilities of doing. One thing I know: God will not call anyone to accomplish anything that he has not given them the capabilities and empowerment to fulfill. He does not call people so He can make fools of them. He calls people so that He can make them successful and victorious through His power and might! He calls. He enables. He empowers. He releases His kids to do His work in His kingdom and become more than conquerors in any and every arena He calls them to. Wow! Life doesn't get any more exciting than that!

3) Once you have recognized a need and know you have the abilities to fill the need, the next step is to begin to use those abilities and refine them in preparation for the task, while at the same time discovering new abilities along the way. You just know God has DESIGNED you for this, but it is up to you to allow Him to perfect His design in you. You might consider this the practice session, where you start to get your feet wet. You find a similar need close at home and see what you can do about it.

Maybe the long-term need you see is to teach English in a country that is closed to Christian missionaries, but wants English teachers for their educational system so as to better prepare their next generation for a broader impact in the world. You know you have teaching abilities, but you have never taught young children before. Why not volunteer at a local elementary school or apply to be a teacher's aide? Maybe you could volunteer at your local public library to read to children. You can even volunteer to teach Sunday School at the elementary level. You will not only have a better grasp on what your abilities are but be able to recognize your weaknesses in that area and work on improving them. Contact the appropriate government agency in the country you are interested in and see what degree you will need and, if necessary, enroll in college and start working toward that degree.

Do not allow discouragement or impatience to take over at this stage. Anything worth doing is worth preparing for, waiting for and being able to do well. Know that when God is in it, He will prepare the way.

4) It seems that once we make our DETERMINATION to follow a call, God always uses people and events along the way to confirm the call to us. I am thinking of a young man who really had talents in the field of playing musical instruments, but always felt incompetent when it came to singing. He began to see the need for contemporary Christian music for the youth in his country and felt such a strong desire to pursue being a worship leader. He determined he would start singing in small churches he could visit and offer his services to evangelists he knew. He had several invitations to sing, and to his amazement, at the first several places he went to minister, he was greatly complimented – not on his instrumental abilities, but on his vocal renditions! That only served to confirm his call and determination.

You see, our self-gratification and success really are not at all important. The all-consuming importance is that God be glorified through each of us to the extent the world will see Him – not us – in all that we accomplish. That doesn't mean that He won't fulfill us and give us success as we live out the desires of our hearts; He will! But that is not what we seek. That is only a by-product of our sincere desire to fulfill the call He has placed upon our lives. What I can guarantee is that you are your happiest only when you are in the center of His will!

5) Finally, it all comes together as the Lord opens the right doors at the right time for us to step into the fulfillment of our DESTINY, or our call. We can make all the plans and preparations, have all the necessary abilities, be overly anxious and willing. But until the right doors are opened at the right time, we will have to content ourselves with sitting back and waiting – patiently! My youngest daughter was given a word from a lovely Christian lady that is so very true: God doesn't waste time or talent! There is nothing of more monumental importance than being in the middle of God's divine timing, position and location. All your well-laid plans will come to naught if you step outside His plan. At the same time, nothing will ever compare to the joy and excitement of serving when you are in the center of His will.

I have known individuals who felt a passion for a particular field in a particular country and then spent several years preparing; at times they totally forgot about their original plan due to the time that had elapsed and just life happening – only to have the doors open down the road for them to do exactly what they had dreamed of doing and prepared to do years before.

These five steps of advice can apply to basically every area of your life. Read them over again, expand them through your own study of the Word and prayer, turn to other reliable resources and people who can add more substance to these basic bones, and GO FOR IT! God does have a call on your life and He, more than even you, wants you to fulfill it. DISCOVER, DESIRE, DESIGN, DETERMINATION, DESTINY!

Early on we recognized that although our girls were missionary kids, they were not the ones called. We had the call, they had no option but to go along. We loved them being involved in our ministry to the extent any Christian parents want their children to grow up involved in church. But our prayer was always that we would raise them in a way that would allow them to recognize and fulfill their own calling – and they (you, my kids) did!

· VIII ·

On Our Way to Save the World!

"Success is making a difference in the lives of others;
happiness is watching them grow because of it."

Meanwhile…following our farewells from Washington, by mid-September 1967 we were living in Guadalajara, Mexico where Mike was to study Spanish. Our trip was interesting and somewhat daring. We had a friend drive us and all our belongings to National City (near San Diego) where we spent a couple of days with Steve and Nancy Harris. They would then drive us into Tijuana where we would catch our flight to Guadalajara. However, on the morning we went to catch our flight, we were told it had been delayed so we returned to their home and finally got word we would fly out that night. Oh – and did I mention that all this time I had been carrying Mike's 45 in Brenda's diaper bag? He wanted to have it for safety in Mexico! The diaper bag was never checked once – thank goodness!

For me, Mexico was a time of enjoying my little girl, taking some translation courses, cooking for one of the professors who joined us for our noon meal each day and, in general, enjoying life in Guadalajara. Brenda was introduced to tortillas, mariachis, sun-laced Saturday breakfasts on the balcony of a restaurant overlooking the rose gardens of one of Guadalajara's beautiful avenues, and – most importantly – to Spanish. Mike was introduced to the horror of Spanish verbs! But we all prospered in our various activities, enjoyed the cute colonial-style bungalow we lived in and the beauty of the city. While in Guadalajara I met the pastor who many years before had dedicated me to the Lord in Ohio. He was pastoring an inter-denominational English church in Guadalajara, which we happened to visit and thus met him. It is indeed a small world!

****

After the nine-month study term, we returned to the States; Brenda and I traveled a little before Mike. I was nicely dressed for the trip and I had her turned out like a little doll. Upon reaching customs in LAX, there was a very hippie-looking young man in front of us, looked a bit high and carried a huge duffel bag. The customs agent barely glanced at his passport and motioned him on through without having to clear customs. When I reached the agent, he studied our passports, studied us, then had us go through a thorough search where they even pulled undeveloped film from its cartridge. You would have thought we were the wild looking ones. I was really upset! Maybe he was looking for that 45...but this time it returned in our one large crate.

Mike caught up with us a couple of days later with what few household effects we had taken to Guadalajara and we headed for Oregon to take Brenda to my grandparents' home where my parents were staying while on furlough. Other than a quick trip I had made to Ecuador (where they were then stationed) for Brenda's second birthday, my parents had not been able to enjoy their only grandchild. So it was that, with some trepidation, we left Brenda with them while we embarked on a two-month itinerary prior to leaving for Panamá, where we had been appointed to serve.

During the months of June and July of 1968, we saw the inside of more churches than most people ever hope to see in a lifetime! At most of them, we were warmly welcomed and treated with wonderful love. At a few, we felt like we were intruding and were happy to present our cause and move right along.

At one church in particular, we were clearly unwanted. They assured us they had not been advised of our arrival; but while changing for the evening service in what was their home office, we found the letter advising them of our plans crumpled up in the wastebasket! As with most places we visited, we were to stay in the pastors' home after the Sunday evening service. However, their "unwelcome mat" was so obvious that after the evening service Mike told the pastors we had decided to go ahead and move on to our next destination that same night. They then argued with us that Monday was a free day for us and we had no business wasting money on a motel. Mike thanked them for their advice, we walked to our loaded car and left.

They were right on one count, money was scarce and we were not enthusiastic about spending additional money on a motel, but sometimes one's sanity is more important than one's finances and you just do what you have to do! And we missed our little girl horribly – especially on that night. But overall, the itinerary experience was a learning, growing, maturing time for us and a beautiful gift for my parents to be able to spend time with Brenda. Because of those months of sharing our mission with others, we felt much more a part of the wider Foursquare mission program when we left for Panamá.

In early August we returned to Oregon to pack what had been left in storage at my grandparents while we were in Mexico, to purchase items we could foresee needing over the next five years, visit relatives to say good-byes and head for Los Angeles, where we greatly anticipated our first trip to the "Alabaster House." This was a supply center stocked by women of our denomination throughout the country, with household articles for missionaries to take with them when leaving for the country of their assignment. I had been there before, but as a missionary kid. Now I was the missionary!

On one of our last days in Oregon, my mother, grandmother, Brenda and I went for a final shopping spree. At some point during the day we passed a nickel machine that had little rings in it, and Brenda wanted one. My mother gave her the required coin, and Brenda watched the ring roll out and proudly put it on her finger. Our next stop was a rather exclusive dress shop where I was hunting for a "good dress" to wear for the farewell dinner in Woodburn, then in Los Angeles, and one that would serve me for important occasions over the next few years. Brenda was showing off her ring to the sales lady, who asked her, "Oh, are you going steady?" To which my matter-of-fact almost three year-old responded, "No! I am going to Panamá!" Obviously, we had to explain to the lady what Brenda was talking about;

but it did get me a nice "missionary" discount and I was able to afford two dresses!

Although I had always watched my parents pack all their earthly goods in barrels for shipping, I had never really packed them myself. Mike and I discovered you CAN put square objects through round holes, and the law of volume or area does not apply to the packing of missionary barrels.

Panamá – The Good, the Bad and the Ugly!

"God never takes you to something He can't bring you through."

I could say that our excitement upon arriving in Panamá in late October of 1968 out-weighed the rough spots we encountered – but I would be lying! We were to take up residence in a little…little being the key word here…second-floor, one-bedroom apartment overlooking the canal in Colón, Panamá. The three of us shared the little bedroom. The kitchen was so small there was only room for one person at a time to be in it, and the remaining area was a small living/dining room that held a couch, two chairs, coffee table, dining table and 6 chairs, buffet, desk, bookcase. The only way to navigate the area was by sidling by the various pieces of furniture.

We had left beautiful fall weather only to arrive in the middle of a hot, humid rainy season. Brenda soon developed a serious heat rash all over her body, including on her face. I determined that the coolest place for her to sleep would be under the open window in the front room that faced the street and the canal, so we set up her cot there. To my utter dismay, the first morning she slept there she awoke covered in soot from the ships that had sailed past in the night! She spent many hours playing in the bath tub filled with water with baking soda in the attempt to dry up the rash and keep her cool at the same time.

After less than a month in our "digs," I had reached my limits. I got up one morning and told Mike he would have to watch Brenda for the day; I was going to go house/apartment hunting and would not be back until I found a place. He reluctantly agreed, but we both knew we couldn't take Brenda out to walk all over the city in the heat. So, after praying together, I set off.

I found several places that were not an option. As I started for home late that afternoon, disheartened and exhausted, I just felt led to walk down a particular street and as I came to a new-looking building, I noticed a young lady putting out an "Apartment for Rent" sign. I ran up to her, asked to see it, and made a verbal agreement on the spot to rent it. It was a four-unit complex, two downstairs apartments, two upstairs; the owners lived in the back downstairs unit and the one available was the front, second story unit. It was perfect…a large kitchen/dining area, comfortably sized living room with a wide balcony running the width of it, two bedrooms, one of them quite large, and a bathroom with hot water.

By the time I rushed back to tell Mike of my find, I had already – mentally – re-upholstered the old front room furniture, pictured the drapes and curtains I would make, and basically had the new apartment decorated. We would take the smaller room and divide the larger one into two areas, one area for Brenda's room and the other area for office space. We started moving within a couple of days and I carried out all my decorating plans within a few weeks. We had a home!

And soon I realized I was pregnant! (This time my persistent cravings were for Chinese food, which was fine as there was a great restaurant run by the Canal Zone right close to home.) Due to the extreme heat, I began having episodes of very low blood pressure, passing out frequently, once downtown on the sidewalk. This inconvenience continued to hassle me until our permanent move back to the US, when I slowly developed high blood pressure...go figure.

Our work in Panamá consisted of working the missionary out of a job and seeing that the church building project in Colón was completed. Mike traveled into the interior by car (if you could call the consistently broken down VW van we had a car!), canoe, bus and horseback or mule. He also became very well acquainted with many items he had never eaten before – or since...armadillo, alligator, monkey...to name a few of the ones he knew what they were! I was "privileged" to try armadillo and alligator, but never had the honor of the others.

On the local scene, we oversaw the completion of a church building, taught in the Bible Institute, Mike preached often, and I became involved with the women's ministry. On a national scale, we fulfilled any duties assigned to us. It was a good time, people came to know the Lord, and we saw God perform some great miracles in the lives and bodies of people.

One outstanding miracle was a young man who entered the church in the middle of the service, very high on drugs and basically out of it. At the close, he raised his hand to accept the Lord; following his repeating the sinner's prayer, he was totally normal, walked home and became a vital member of the youth group. During our time in Panamá we also discovered that our input into leaders was something of great value to young ministers, as well as an avenue of great fulfillment to us. That aspect of ministry would be our forte for many years to come.

During the months leading up to our baby's birth, Brenda became very ill with a kidney infection. The Panamanian doctors we took her to, didn't seem to be able to diagnose the problem. Not being military, we had no privileges in the Canal Zone; however, there was a military family who rented the apartment right behind us, and he was an Army doctor from New York. This was in the early Vietnam era, and the special Green Beret troops trained in Panamá, as weather conditions were very comparable to what they would face upon deployment to Vietnam.

I went to Dr. Cohen and begged, pleaded, ranted, and raged until he agreed to take Brenda to the military clinic to run some studies. The doctors there immediately found the problem and agreed to perform the minor intervention needed to remedy it. To this day, I don't know how they agreed to do this, but our "Commander-in-Chief" is undoubtedly higher in rank than the top commander of their military post! Brenda never had problems of that nature again.

On the evening of December 13, 1969, I decorated our home for Christmas, standing on chairs to string lights along the balcony, lifting Brenda to put the star at the top of the tree and doing what I could with what I had. The next morning, I was on my way to the hospital and on December 14th our second daughter, Leahna Jeanelle, delighted our lives with her arrival. She was an impatient little girl and made her appearance only three minutes after the doctor made his! We were all very excited and four-year old Brenda welcomed her baby sister enthusiastically.

One afternoon I was occupied in the house and realized I had not seen Brenda for a while and began calling her. There was no answer, so I began a search of the apartment with no results. I became quite concerned and walked out on the big balcony that ran across the front of the apartment. I kept calling her, and finally got up enough nerve to approach the railing and look over the balcony, dreading what I might see below. Nothing. Just as I was beginning to panic, I looked over at a large cardboard box in the corner against the wall. I walked over to it, peeked inside and there, much to my relief, was my little girl sound asleep with her pillow and teddy bear.

Right around this same time we welcomed a young lady into our home, Barbara Petersen, who was a missionary apprentice. She shared Brenda's "bedroom." She was a lot of fun, great company for me, and we certainly enjoyed her time with us.

When Leahna was seven months old, the swine flu was making its rounds in Panamá. Mike was the first to succumb, then only a day later I came down with it. As tends to happen at times like these, Barb was off in Panamá City working in a Vacation Bible School, so we had no help. I remember literally crawling to the kitchen and pulling myself up to the table to heat a bottle for Leahna, make a sandwich for Brenda and take more liquids to Mike. In a couple of days, he was better so he could take care of me and watch over the girls. We were really sick. But the worse was yet to come.

I had been back on my feet only a few days when Leahna started showing signs of the flu. By that night her temperature was uncontrollable, and we called the clinic where she had been born and rushed her there. If I live to be a thousand, I will never forget looking at my baby girl being placed in a large basin of ice, her teeth chattering as she weakly said, "Mama, mama!" The doctor and nurses on duty knew they had to get her fever down immediately before it caused any permanent brain damage; I knew what they were doing was the correct thing, but my heart simply could not bear it.

Mike and I stood by and prayed, and one of us would slip out of the room from time to time to check on Brenda who had fallen asleep in a big chair in the hallway. Our prayers were answered, Leahna was soon back to her happy, active self, and Brenda never did get the flu; but I have yet to recover from the long night watch as Leahna fought against the elevated fever that threatened her life.

****

One of the greatest confirmations regarding being obedient in praying for people when the Lord places some-one on your mind and heart happened while we lived in Colón. Leahna's crib was in our room, and she would wake up about 4:00 a.m. every morning for a bottle. On one par-ticular Sunday morning, she began to fuss somewhat earlier, about 3:30 a.m. I decided to let her fuss a little and maybe she would go back to sleep, but – just in case – I would go ahead and heat up her bottle and place it in the thermal holder.

As I walked out of our bedroom, I noticed the hallway door leading into the living area was open (we always kept it closed as we had a window air-conditioner in our bedroom and it kept both bedrooms cool). The hallway door was immediately in front of the bathroom, where we left the door open with a night light on for Brenda's sake. I stood silhouetted in the hallway door and looked into the living room at the front door where I saw a man crouched down going through my purse! (My purse had been on top of the laundry hamper inside the hallway by our bedroom door.) He was barefooted, dressed only in what looked like a pair of under shorts, and his body glistened even in the semi-darkness.

Rather than being frightened, I was indignant! How dare this man come into our home and even worse, how dare he be going through my purse? I looked at him, and as he saw me, he remained in his crouched position and watched me. I was standing there in my flimsy nightgown with the nightlight shining behind me from the bathroom. Then I said, "Who do you think you are going through my purse here in my house?" He watched me a few more seconds then jumped over the wall of the balcony/hallway that ran the entire side of the building, giving access to both our apartment and the one behind us.

I ran into our bedroom and woke up Mike (the sound sleeper of the century), put on a robe and called our landlords downstairs. The two sisters came, and we discovered the intruder had taken out the dining room screen, removed several louvered windows and climbed in the window onto the table. Our landlord decided we needed to call the police immediately, and since they knew someone personally of a high rank on the police force, they called him.

Two officers arrived shortly and began to interview me. They had me go over my story several times while taking notes, then said to me, "Señora, your story all makes sense, except you did not see the man." I repeated that I had, and again reiterated how he was (un) dressed, how his body seemed shiny, how he jumped over the wall. They admitted he had probably greased his body so that he could easily escape by sliding down the wall, but still insisted I had not seen him.

Getting tired of this and not liking being called a liar, I asked them why they did not believe I had seen him. They replied that the exact same thing had happened at an apartment a couple of blocks away earlier that same night... only the lady could not tell her story because when she had surprised the intruder, he had stabbed her to death. A man matching the description I had given had been seen running down the block by a neighbor who had been awake and out on his balcony at the time.

Quite unnerved, we didn't quite know what to say to that, but were advised by the officers not to mention the event to anyone at church as so many people came and went there, it was possible the thief was someone who knew us and might do or say something that would give himself away. We obliged, and actually didn't even go to church that Sunday morning. Mike had just returned from a trip and didn't have any responsibilities that morning, so we decided to stay home and calm our nerves.

A few weeks later I was getting ready to leave church for home when a little elderly lady of the congregation stopped me. She looked at me closely and said, "Sister Lolita, how have you been? Have you been alright?" I could tell she was deeply concerned about me, so I took time to assure her I was indeed fine, we were all fine. She just shook her head, but I could still see she had questions. "Why do you ask?"

She looked at me with her fading eyesight and told me an incredible story. "About three weeks ago, at around 3:30 on a Sunday morning, I was awakened by a frightening dream. I saw a front door standing wide open and the entrance mat was all shredded and covered in blood. Your name kept resonating in my mind. I didn't know what to do; I was shaking violently I was so afraid. So, I did the only thing I knew to do...I got out of bed and knelt down and prayed for you and your family."

Now I was shaking violently – not from fear, but by the awesome realization that this faithful servant of the Lord's had been at the throne of God on my behalf at a moment I so desperately needed God's protection! I still get goose bumps when I think about or relate this incident. Never, Never, NEVER brush off a sense that you need to pray for someone – it could literally be a matter of life and death! *"You are my hiding place; You shall preserve me from trouble; You shall surround me with songs of deliverance."* Psalm 32:7.

Around mid 1969, we wrote a letter to the Mission Board to ask if any thoughts or determinations were being made regarding plans for our future. We had been told we would only be in Panamá for two years, and those two years were quickly coming to an end.

In rather short order, we received a response. They offered three countries they would like us to pray about... one of them was Argentina; I don't remember the other two.

And we really had no need to do much praying; that had been settled in our hearts in San Pedro Sula better than five years earlier; we already knew it was our God-led destiny! So, we responded and before long were in the process of working on the required documentation for a move. We had enjoyed our time in Panamá but were really ready to settle into what we felt would be a long-term assignment.

As the documentation was taking longer than anticipated, Missions requested that we transfer to Ecuador for a few months while the paperwork was being completed. Daddy was supervisor of the Ecuador work at that time, and Mommy pastored the huge Central Church in Guayaquil. The Foursquare work there was in the midst of establishing by-laws and registering with the government; it was a very difficult process which Daddy was caught in the middle of and had even received some serious threats. Missions felt we could be an encouragement to my parents, Mike could travel with Daddy for the sake of protection, we could minister to the people, and also glean wisdom for the time when the same process of registering the church with the government would need to be done in Argentina.

We packed up our barrels, had farewell events, packed two suitcases and two carry-on bags for each of us, tourist visas for Ecuador were applied for and received. Good-bye time came quickly, and we became acutely aware of how many people in Panamá had stolen our hearts. We would miss them, and some of the culture as well...nacatamales, chicheme, arroz con pollo, sea breezes, palm tree lined beaches...but we were glad to leave the constant hot weather behind!

****

Ecuador was a decidedly interesting time. The fact that we could spend time with my parents, brother and sister was delightful, occasional time at the beach was great, and ministry time was rewarding. We were able to visit many areas of the country and add some important lessons to our experience as missionaries. However, the grinding work of by-laws, board meetings – a few very difficult ones – government laws and a few threatening board members, could have easily deterred our attention from the positive. God was at work, and the enemy was not happy about it!

A most memorable trip was one I made with Daddy to the town of Machala. It brought back so many memories of trips I had made with him as a child in Honduras and was truly a wonderful opportunity. He and I left Guayaquil late one evening on a boat, a very loaded down boat! We had "berths," if you could call them that...a narrow sector with a few of hammocks. We arrived in Machala in the late hours of the night – or was it the wee hours of the morning? It was rainy season and we literally sunk into mud up to our knees as we walked from the landing pier to seek a non-existent taxi. I remember worrying about Daddy; he was carrying my accordion, which made him be even more weighted down. As he was diabetic, my concern was for any cuts on his feet or legs that might become infected. But gratefully, that didn't happen, even though we had to walk all the way to the church parsonage.

We finally reached the pastors' home, where a good shower, a wonderful hot meal (Was it a midnight supper or early breakfast? Who knows or cares!) and then real beds awaited us. OK, so it was a roughly made bed frame with an extremely thin mattress, but it had a clean sheet and a pillow, so all was well. We stayed a couple of days, God showed up to do some great miracles, I sang my heart out just for the pure delight of it, both alone and with Daddy, and we both preached and taught the two days and nights we were there...very moving, very wonderful!

We also experienced another type of moving while we were in Guayaquil: the household was awakened by a serious earthquake around 3:00 one morning. My parents' house was large, several bedrooms, large living and dining rooms, office, maid quarters, three bathrooms, all which made for many doorways. One would think there would be enough doorways for all the nine people living in the house, but evidently not – we all ended up trying to jam under the same doorway, which is supposed to be a safe spot! Thankfully, no one was hurt, there were some slight wall cracks in the house, major cracks in sidewalks and the street in front of the house; but several weeks later Mommy was alone one night and heard a horrendous crash. One whole wall of kitchen cupboards had fallen to the floor, obviously loosened by that earthquake. She lost a lot of dishes! This experience gave a whole new meaning to Psalm 46:2-3, *"Therefore we will not fear, even though the earth be removed, and though the mountains be carried into the midst of the sea; Though its waters roar and be troubled, though the mountains shake with its swelling."* This verse has held truth and hope during spiritual shakings as well.

While in Ecuador we celebrated Brenda's fifth birthday on November 23rd – big party – and then Leahna's first birthday on December 14th. She walked for the first time that day and was very proud of herself! Next came a big Christmas celebration, rather bitter-sweet as we knew it would be the last Christmas we would all spend together for who-knew-how-long. But the necessary documents had finally come through for us, and two days after Christmas, December 27th, 1970, we boarded a Braniff flight from Guayaquil, Ecuador to Buenos Aires, Argentina.

· X ·

New Beginnings

*"No matter what feelings I have about today,
I've learned to keep in mind that it really doesn't
matter; after all, it is the Lord's day!"*

If I had to describe our Argentine years, I would say
they were intense. Life in Argentina in the seventies and
eighties was not only intense, but lusty, bold, passionate,
and constantly in political turmoil. From the simple country life to the bustling metropolis, daily living was highly
emotional. At times I felt as if I needed a protective shield
just to be able to breath calmly in the midst of the constant
turmoil and upheavals we were faced with. And yet it was
invigorating, exciting and held a sort of magical sway over
one. In retrospect, it was like living in a fantasy land where
everything happened on an exaggerated level. But those
will forever be the best and happiest, most productive years
of my life.

Our arrival at Ezeiza International Airport was an
exciting moment for us – we had finally arrived at the land
of our calling and our expectations and anticipations ran
high. It was a hot muggy day...as bad as the hot weather

we had just left in Ecuador, but it was summertime on that end of the world and at least we had on the right clothes for the weather. After finally clearing immigration and luggage inspection – all eight suitcases and eight carry-on bags – we required two cabs, and with a lot of juggling were able to get all of us in a cab and the luggage loaded in the second one. All we had was an address; in a city of thirteen million people, we had no idea where we were going, how to get there, or how much it should cost us for the cabs. But we were blessed in that the cab drivers were patient and honest.

On our more than an hour drive from the airport, our driver also served as tour guide and gave us valuable information about the various neighborhoods we traveled through, such as the strange method of streets in each neighborhood having the same names as streets in other neighborhoods. He also gave us a few cultural lessons. It was Sunday afternoon, and along the highways there were many large park areas where thousands were out picnicking, playing soccer or just drinking their afternoon mate. It all looked very foreign to us. And the people all looked very European…we were confused, hot, tired, and jet-lagged!

We arrived in the suburb of San Isidro at around 4:00 that Sunday afternoon, to the rented house where the previous missionary had lived (Dr. and Mrs. Vinton Johnson), only to find it locked up with no one in sight to meet us, although a telegram had been sent to the pastor of the local church who also acted as president of the country's national Foursquare church board. I am sure we provided quite a sight for the neighbors…all dressed up (you "dressed" to travel in those days), exhausted, two little girls that were no longer having fun, and all of us were hungry and thirsty.

There was a small bakery with a few grocery supplies next door to the house, and it opened at 6:00 p.m. By that time I was desperate. Leahna's milk supply for her bottle was depleted, and both girls were fussy from hunger...so were Mike and I, only we couldn't/shouldn't cry in public. I went next door and introduced myself as their new neighbor, telling them our predicament. The shop owners were so warm and friendly. I explained that I had no Argentine money, but she insisted I take some bread and sweet rolls, cold cuts she had in her own refrigerator, and a quart of milk she also had. Milk was not delivered on Sundays, so she shared her own supply. She said I could pay her whenever, and to be sure and come back for anything else I might need. Her husband knew someone close by that knew the pastor and sent word that we had arrived.

I was so grateful I nearly started to cry, but rushed back to the house, and we all sat on suitcases in the front yard while I fashioned some sandwiches that we ate together, giving each of the girls some milk. By then we were all so totally spent, we could have cared less what the neighbors or cars passing by thought of us!

It was well after 8:00 p.m. when the pastor's wife finally showed up with keys to the house. She was friendly – but not overly so. We began to drag all our possessions into the house, which had been empty and closed up for nearly two months. The humidity was awful, the heat overwhelming, there was mold everywhere and the air was stale. There was nothing in the refrigerator, but fortunately there was electricity and I was able to put the remainder of our picnic supplies away.

The next thing we did was to open every available window to try and let some fresh air in…how were we to know it was the height of mosquito season? Of course, there were no screens. Mike and I removed sheets from our large duffel bag that held most all the household effects we would have until our shipment arrived, which could be anywhere from six weeks to six months. We pulled a mattress into the largest bedroom for the girls to sleep on, then took turns at an all-night vigil of fanning the girls as they slept to keep them somewhat cooled off and keep the mosquitoes away. It was not the best night of our lives!

The early morning hours provided some release from the heat, and either the mosquitos had taken their fill or were also resting in the cool morning air. It seemed we had just settled into a quiet time of rest when the doorbell rang. Mike was in his undershorts, so I quickly pulled on a housedress I had on top of a suitcase and went to answer the door.

I peeked out, and the man that stood there said, "I am the Rev. So-and So, pastor of the local church, head of the Bible Institutes and President of the Foursquare Board of Directors. Welcome to Argentina!"

I did not feel welcomed by this proud, unfeeling man! Half asleep, the other half zoned out, I replied, "Thank you; I am Sister Lolita." I explained our situation, the sleepless night, and exhaustion, and asked if there was a possibility he might return later in the morning or that afternoon. He acted somewhat disgruntled but agreed to come back later that day. Of course, by then, the girls were awake, and once he left we started on an inspection of our new home.

What we found was a small settee, two uncomfortable parlor chairs and a book shelf in the front room; a double bed, an armoire and desk in the room behind that one; then came the small bathroom, then a room with two single beds and another armoire, and behind that room a small room with a table and six chairs. The last room was the kitchen, and what a shock that was! Two cracked plates, as many knives, forks and spoons, a blackened tea kettle and three or four cans of various sizes that were obviously intended as kettles. Oh yeah, there was a spatula, two large spoons, a large fork and a tray with two glasses and four teacups on it. On the back porch I found a broom, a mop and bucket, and discovered we were now the proud owners of a tomcat! How he had survived, I have no idea, but he mewed until I gave him some watered down milk from my precious supply and a hunk of bread. We didn't even like cats!!! The house was of the style known as a "sausage house," one long narrow building on a deep, narrow lot, one room after another, in train-like style. It did have a great back yard, which was indeed a blessing for the girls.

The first thing on the agenda was to get some cleaning supplies, so I again went next door to our neighbors, only to find the store closed; bakeries were all closed on Mondays. The lady was just leaving, and when I told her what I needed, she let me in to pick up a few items. She also suggested a couple of things she had that would make a lunch for us and gave me some left over sweet rolls from the previous day's bake. I added a box of tea and another quart of milk to the small pile, stopped at the green grocer's for fruit at the corner that also accepted my pay-you-later explanation, then went back to attack the house.

We cleaned frantically until nearly noon; I cooked some pasta and veggies in our fancy can-kettles, and we all took a nap. Our welcome committee returned that afternoon, including the important Rev. Pastor/Director/President (Mr. PDP), another pastor who really was nice, a young lady, Eliana Muñoz (now Caudillo), who would become my bosom buddy once she stopped growling at me, and her mother, Tella Muñoz, who became the beloved nanny to my girls. This time we were prepared – I even made tea and had some pastries! Mike and I drank the tea iced and used the cups to serve our guests proper hot tea. Some basic plans were made, including a trip to the metropolis the next day for us to get some money exchanged and be able to start the process of settling in. Tella offered to bring us a few more dishes to eat from, which I gladly accepted.

Over the next few weeks, we became acquainted with several pastors, attended the local church, made a few friends and found someone to drive Mike around to visit some of the churches. There was a Jeep pickup (made in Argentina with a Torino engine) for us when we arrived, and after having some work done on it due to it having been sitting for sometime, it proved a worthy vehicle. Also, we had visitors during those first rough weeks, a missionary couple from Brazil, Gary and Leslie Royer. They were like a breath of fresh air to us, and when they left, we felt much better about life in general.

Finally, after about three months, our shipment arrived. By then we had rented a different house, same neighborhood, but much more "homey" and adaptable to our family. We painted, unpacked, and settled in for the long haul. I wanted the small kitchen painted in pale yellow with light blue accents. One of the young men from the church that was helping us commented on the colors and asked me if we were "de Boca." I had no idea what he was talking about, but he quickly explained that the best soccer team in Argentina was the Boca team. He said it was the team of the common people, and its colors were blue and yellow. Sounded good to me, we shook hands, and our whole family has been "de Boca" ever since! A very small over-the-garage room was painted pink and we were able to find two small beds that would serve the girls, we ordered some front room furniture and it wasn't long before all four of us were beginning to feel settled and ready to face life in a somewhat normal fashion.

In the meantime, I had found a kindergarten for Brenda, "Story Land," in the suburb next to our own, Acassuso. It proved to be a fantastic choice and Brenda thrived. It had only one major drawback…a teacher who was enamored with Mike and openly flirted with him in my presence. I am guessing my glares in her direction plus our hanging on one another like newly-weds, finally gave her a clue!

Those first weeks and months were filled with first impressions, new experiences, and much learning! Mike was busy trying to meet as many of the forty or so pastors throughout the country, so he traveled a lot. The work was on shaky grounds due to Mr. PDP, and it was imperative that Mike become known and learn the ropes as quickly as possible. But let me just share a few observations of that early time frame from my personal point of view…

Everywhere else I had lived, nylons (subsequently becoming pantyhose) were not only common but mandatory for any dress-up occasions, such as church, meetings, or trips to down-town. And, being the well-groomed lady that I was, I had always complied. Well, after the first few times of being out and about while dressed up, I had become paranoid because people stared at my legs. OK – I am not bragging here, but I will admit my legs were pretty shapely back then, but there seemed to be more to it than that, because it was the women more than the men that stared! I finally got up enough nerve to ask Eliana; she laughed and informed me that no one ever wore nylons in the summer, but that I really did need to tan my legs. And I did!

I learned four things in short order about the Argentine women...you could never be too thin, too tanned, too blond or too sophisticated! And believe me, those women had it all under control! I have never known more beautiful, sophisticated, elegant women. I worked on that a lot, but never quite succeeded. I was always just a little too robust, never quite tan enough, and enjoyed life too much to worry a lot about the sophistication part...I have always preferred to just be me. But I was blonde! (I am generally considered as a classy lady, so it's OK!)

The Argentine people in general are simply beautiful people, well groomed, well mannered and the vast majority of them very well-read and intelligent.

Then there was the unique cultural event of "Mate." My first experience was not good. It was served to me by Eliana (before she stopped growling) and tasted just plain nasty! But soon I had a second experience, served by someone who had taken a liking to me, and I was hooked for life. From that point on it has been a staple at our house, to the extent that we were held up in airport customs one time when returning to the USA because we had several packets of the yerba mate tea in our suitcases and the inspectors had to make sure it was a legal weed!

One of the most challenging realizations was that things I had known the names for in any other country were called something different in Argentina. Green beans, pineapple, cuts of meat, grapefruit, cabbage, butter, underwear items, baby bottles, and on and on, all had me baffled for awhile. A few experiences stand out in this regard.

We went into a fruit drink/malt shop during our first few days there, and after the waiter named off several options for fruit smoothies, I proceeded to ask for "piña (pineapple)." The waiter smiled, and said, "Señora, are you sure you want a piña?" to which I responded in the positive. "Are you real sure you want a piña?" Now I was becoming leery. "I think so." He proceeded to make a fist and punched the air with it, while laughingly telling me that was a "piña" in Argentina. Pineapple was known as "ananá." Lesson learned.

Then there was my shopping expedition to have some metal eyelets placed on a little pair of rompers I had made for Leahna. I went to several sewing supply shops… each type of merchandise has its own specialty shop there… asking for "ojetes dorados." I thought I was asking for golden eyelets, but at each shop I was looked at strangely, giggled at, and one lady just looked at me hatefully. Finally, I was told by the lady at the fourth shop that they were called "ojalillos dorados." I made the mistake of inquiring what I had been asking for and was mortified to learn I had been asking for golden buttholes! Lesson learned.

Wanting to purchase some Italian style sausage at the meat market, I wasn't sure how they sold it; I asked the butcher and he straight-faced told me that it was by the meter.

I ordered a half meter while other shoppers around me snickered. The butcher then told me it was sold by the kilo, like all other meat. Lesson learned. Incidentally, over time I also learned that being a comedian seemed to be a prerequisite to being a butcher!

The first time I needed to buy a new bra, I asked for a "brasier," only to discover that what I actually wanted was a "corpiño." I soon found that most of my clothing items had somehow undergone name changes when I moved to Argentina, and after being offered men's underwear in my search for girls' panties, I always asked someone I knew the name of whatever it was I needed before going shopping. Lesson learned.

After about the first month, Eliana decided I could be trusted, and we began to develop a very strong friendship that continues until this day. Our first immediate discovery is that we both loved to sing, and sing we did...all over Buenos Aires, then all over Argentina, and ultimately in other countries as well. And we also found another common ground – we loved a good laugh! Whenever we were together the air would ring with boisterous laughter. We have had a lot of fun together, despite some of the rougher moments we have shared. Eliana quickly became a confidante for me and surrogate aunt to my girls. She would often come and stay with us when Mike traveled, which was of great help. We still talk – and laugh – by phone and e-mail regularly. We have been blessed to be able to see each other about once a year, and those are very special times.

We acquired a boxer pup shortly after our arrival who was, for whatever reason, extremely jealous of Eliana. One morning after she had spent the night with the girls and me, we awoke to find her shoes chewed beyond recognition. Not good. The next destruction happened when I had been ironing outside because there was a cool breeze, and while I ran into the house for something, Duke yanked on the iron cord and began to swing it around like a lasso, breaking the iron to smithereens. Not good. Then we noticed that the not-so-small fruit trees in our back yard were being completely demolished, again, by Duke. Not good. He loved the girls and wanted to play with them constantly, but he was now becoming larger and his attempt at playing with them would leave them knocked over in the grass. Not good.

However, he loved pacifiers! Leahna was addicted to them and every time Duke would get one, she would be devastated, but little by little her collection of pacifiers was disappearing until she was down to just one. Good! She finally had to toss that one as well once Duke got it. Let me just say, if you have never seen a boxer happily sucking on a pacifier, you have not lived! In the end, we gave Duke to our meat market owner who treated him like a king and fed him like one as well.

During the first fall in Buenos Aires (March – May 1971) we spent a lot of time coming and going to official offices, securing our permanent residence papers. It was no small feat, and at times we were exasperated to the point of tears, but we finally were all full-fledged residents of Argentina. Next was procuring our drivers' licenses. What we thought would be a nightmare turned out to be an easy task, both of us being issued licenses to drive all types of vehicles, including trucks and motorcycles!

All too soon our first Buenos Aires winter was upon us. Think cold, damp, humid, and no central heat. Add to that the fact that I had very little experience with cold weather, especially where my girls were concerned, and you will understand why we spent that first winter suffering from colds, flu, and smelling of Vick's during most of the season. The house we had rented had an oil heater at the entrance way, which did serve to take the chill off, but the fumes of which also gave us severe headaches. I was taught to set a pan of water filled with eucalyptus leaves on top of the heater, which did help with the fumes but added to the humidity. We would all go to bed dressed in several layers of pajamas, robes, sweaters, whatever, then wake up and watch our breath form that tell-tale freezing fog as we exhaled. Spring had never been so excitedly anticipated by anyone as it was by us at the end of that first winter!

A few months after our arrival, Mr. PDP decided to split the Foursquare work, thinking he would keep the majority of churches and pastors for his own organization, leaving Foursquare with only a small number. Much to his chagrin, the opposite happened. Of the some thirty churches and meeting places, nine went with him and the rest remained faithful to the Foursquare denomination. The whole episode was enormously difficult and painful, particularly for Mike. In his letter of resignation from Foursquare, Mr. PDP had listed some twenty-eight reasons for leaving the organization, twenty-five of them being blamed on Mike...he hadn't even been in the country long enough to do a fourth of the things of which he was being accused!

And here was where it was so important that we were grounded in the destiny of our calling. If ever we felt like simply walking away and admitting we had made a mistake, and felt we were not cut out for the long haul, it was during that time. We never actually voiced that sentiment, but deep down we felt it – and much later admitted having had those feelings. Had we not known without a doubt that Argentina was indeed our God-given destiny, our history – and to a great extent the Foursquare history of Argentina – this would be a completely different story.

As we prayed, cried, and consulted together, we found a scripture that became our life's ministry verse: Galatians 6:9, *"And let us not grow weary while doing good, for in due season we shall reap if we do not lose heart."* Little did we know at the time when that verse became "ours," that it would be several years before we saw the great revival and outpouring from God that we labored toward! However, once the split was in the past and things began to fall into their rightful place, we felt we could seriously have an effect on training and mentoring, both in the Bible Institute and through one-on-one relationships.

****

Early spring of the next year, I received a phone call from some long-time friends of my parents who said they were in a particular hotel in Buenos Aires and would love to see us. Mike was traveling and would not be back for a couple more days, but I immediately got in touch with Eliana to come stay with the girls and took the train, then subway, downtown to the lovely hotel where they were staying. As I entered their room, they were just extremely excited. They hugged me and giggled and kept glancing at one another…I was excited too, but…seriously? They seemed a bit over the top. Then one of them opened the bathroom door…and out popped my parents! Now I was over the top! They had paid my parents' way to come from Ecuador with them and my parents were able to spend two wonderful weeks with us. It was indeed a much-needed boost to our spirits, and they were a great encouragement to us. Of course, Brenda and Leahna were very excited to have Grandma and Grandpa there and received some extra spoiling those couple of weeks.

As Brenda's first semester of kindergarten came to a close, I knew it was time to seek out a school where the girls could attend long term. Together with another American friend, Judy Davis, whose husband headed up Bank of America in Argentina, we began to visit bilingual schools in our area. We did our homework well, speaking with head-masters and headmistresses, sitting in classrooms, chatting with teachers, reading about the different schools' histories and observing the children.

After many long days of school shopping, the Davis family decided to send their children to the (one and only) American school, The Lincoln School. We made our decision in favor of St. Andrews Scots School, an early Presbyterian institution, the oldest bilingual school of the western hemi-sphere. It was undoubtedly the most decisive, positive deci-sion we ever made in regard to our daughters' education and future success in life. I enrolled Brenda immediately for the following semester for her to start first grade. She was on a waiting list, but after taking the entrance exam (yes, an entrance exam for first grade!), she was accepted. Once you had a child in the school, all other siblings were afford-ed first choice acceptance, and so it was that the future of all our daughters' schooling was secured. Brenda started to first grade mid February 1972. Shortly thereafter I found I was pregnant with our third child.

One of the pastors who helped "mold" me was an extremely religious person…in the bad sense. The first time he met me, he made it known to anyone that would listen that my skirt was much too short. Of course, I heard about it through the grapevine. Trying to be agreeable, upon being invited to his church for Mike to preach and me to sing, I decided to be very prim. It was winter, so I wore a maxi skirt, which was the in thing that year. Well, he then complained because I was too worldly and dressed in a much too modern fashion.

The final straw occurred on a very warm day the following summer. I had on a pair of Bermuda shorts and a sleeveless blouse while diligently cleaning house. The doorbell rang, and without thinking, I simply answered it…to find Mr. Religious standing there staring at me in my shorts and "sleazy" blouse. I narrowed the gap in the door, told him I did not want to disrespect him, but was busy cleaning house and inappropriately dressed to receive company. I said I was sorry, and to please let us know when it was convenient for him to return. He just smiled big, said he understood, but that I needn't feel disrespectful and if it was OK with me, he would be pleased to come in and wait for my husband – go figure. I learned that the old adage was indeed true, only I paraphrased it a bit: "You can please that pastor some of the time, but you can't please all the pastors all of the time!" I also never quite trusted him after that…

I had become very comfortable shopping at the little neighborhood shops – bakery, green grocers, fresh pasta, meat market and small grocery store. As I was waiting in line at the meat market one day, there was another young lady about my age in line in front of me. I had brought the car as I intended to make several stops and purchases, and the meat market was my last stop of the morning. I noticed she was quite loaded down as well, so when she finished her purchase, I asked if she lived close by. She said yes, just a few blocks away. I offered to give her and all her purchases a ride home, and she gratefully accepted. We immediately discovered she lived right across the street from us.

Her husband was a pilot for Aerolineas Argentinas, they had not been married too long, and had just purchased the house. That was the beginning of an amazing friendship, not only between Ana Ines Mattanó and me, but for our entire families. Over the years we spent many, many hours together, just hanging out by her pool, family dinners, doing art and ceramics together, shopping, cooking, talking about child raising (she and I became pregnant at about the same time, she with her first son, Alan, me with Debra), spending time with each other's parents, and growing more like sisters than friends. It was a sad day when they moved to Italy shortly before our move back to the USA...but our friendship remains firm. She visited us once in Oklahoma, my mother and I visited them in Italy. Probably the deepest, most meaningful letters and e-mails I write or receive are between us.

· XI ·

Falling in Love Again

"Serving feels good, not because others recognize our efforts, but because it makes life more meaningful."

As those early weeks and months passed, I found myself involved in an amazing love affair with Argentina. I loved to travel the countryside and catch little glimpses of lifestyles and customs. I came to simply adore the city of Buenos Aires, its quaint streets and artistic statues, with all its busy movement, little unique corners and neighborhoods, well appointed shops and boutiques filled with designer clothing and fascinating accessories, its beautifully preserved architecture, elegant avenues, famous night spots and historical buildings and monuments. Sometimes the beauty of it all almost hurt.

The folklore from all the different parts of the country was fascinating to me. The local music, epic tales and indigenous works of art of each province simply awed me. The history and life of the gaucho amazed me. Sitting around campfires or kitchen tables drinking mate while sharing life experiences were truly some of the most educational times of my life. Times spent at coffee shops over steaming coffee with some tidbit or other, tea times with friends, be it in well appointed homes, the poorest houses made of adobe in the remote areas, or in luxurious tea rooms of the big cities, it was all so marvelous. I don't know what thrilled me most: participating in these times myself or introducing my daughters to them!

And then there was the tango...its music and its dance. I studied its history, listened to it voraciously, watched the dancing on TV and once in a while had the opportunity to attend a dinner club where tango was the entertainment. As most of you know, my personalized car license plate reads, "O2TANGO," as in, "Oh, to tango,' my way of reminiscing! Strange as it seemed, I soon felt like I was meant to be Argentine, even though I was a recent immigrant. I often think of Dr. Livingston and his request that his heart be buried in Africa; I fully understand.

But most of all, I fell in love with the people, beautiful both inside and out, people of so many extractions. There are the prim and proper British; the colorful, loud Russians; the bold, brazen Spaniards; the rugged, brooding Arabs; the expressive, boisterous Italians; the industrious, austere Israelis; the rather arrogant French; the tough, brusque Germans; many other smaller groups from different European countries; the humble almost forgotten indigenous; the strong, proud Creole – and mixtures of all the above! I have lived in so many places, have friends literally around the world, but by far my all-time favorite people, the ones who have forever stolen my heart, are the Argentines. I may be American by birth, but my heart is definitely Argentine!

There is no doubt that the Argentines are a proud people, and in many ways, rightfully so. They are beautiful, talented, and hard workers. They are well educated, enjoy the arts and their country is a paradise of unbelievably varied geographic and scenic environments. But they also have one great negative trait even they are aware of – and in fact brag about. It is known as the "viveza criolla," best explained as a sly sharpness of an almost primitive nature, innate to the native people (in this case the Argentine) of the land. Although this characteristic can be at times comical or creative, valid, and even necessary for survival, it is very often used for one's personal gain to the detriment of another.

Unfortunately, when in Argentina, do as the Argentines. It did not take me too long to pick up on this nuance, and the next thing I knew I was actually putting it into use. But let me just say in my defense, although I did use it occasionally for my benefit, I did not use is to the detriment of others! In fact, there were times when you had to either sink or swim in the midst of cultural circumstances. Please keep in mind, my hunger for all things cultural had been with me from a very early age, and only grew more avid as the years progressed.

Case in point...the Jeep I previously mentioned had a few detrimental characteristics of its own, and often stalled at the most inopportune times. One such time, I was on the main avenue of San Isidro, in the middle of traffic, and it sputtered to a stop. I sat there with horns blowing, a few hitherto unknown hand salutes being offered in my direction, and had no idea what to do until – tah dah – the viveza criolla kicked in. So, dressed in my probably too tight slacks, I proceeded to open the hood, get out of the truck and climb up to peer into the engine. The first guy to pass me screeched to a stop and offered his help to the young blonde in distress. He wiggled a few wires and asked for my phone number so he could make sure I arrived home safely. I thanked him, told him I had no phone, flashed my wedding ring, got into the truck and drove away. Ahh, such a rewarding experience!

Another time it came into play...not by me, mind you...was when three of my friends and I went to do a little shopping together in San Isidro. I seldom drove there because parking was such an issue, but on this particular day I found what I suspect was the one and only valid parking space left in the entire area. It was right at the end of a block, only a couple of blocks from the main shopping area. So I pulled my small Citroen in behind the last car, leaving about a foot between us so the other car could maneuver its way out if necessary...I had no problem. One of my more notable talents was that I could park on a dime.

A couple of hours later we returned to the car, only to find that yet another car had pulled in behind me, fender to fender, and pushed me fender to fender to the car in front of me. Short of osmosis, there was no way I would get out of that parking space. Two of my friends told me and the third gal to go ahead and get in and they would roll the car behind me back so I could get out. I did as they said, watched them bend down to push the car back, noticed they took them awhile to straighten up, and they then jumped in the car. As we took off, I noticed in my rear-view mirror that not only had the felon's car been left halfway in the middle of the intersection, but both of its front tires were nearly completely flat. In the back seat, Alejandra and Ana Ines were choking from laughter!

That little car was the topic of many episodes. On in particular is when it stalled in the middle of main intersection during a summer flash flood. A torrential rain was falling, I was driving with Eliana in the passenger seat and a visiting pastor – dressed in suit and tie – was in the back seat. Well, Eliana and I took off our shoes, got out and proceeded to push the car out of the water while the pastor sat in the car! I really don't blame him; it was probably his only suit and dress shoes. After I got the car started, we stopped at an ice-cream parlor for much needed refreshment. Eliana and I went in but the pastor would not enter with us as he was embarrassed because we were barefooted! However, he had no problem enjoying the ice-cream cone we brought him to the car!

During our second year there, one of Mike's trips took him to the northern provinces of Chaco and Formosa, where we had a few struggling works among the indigenous people of the Toba and Pilagá tribes. Argentina has only a three percent population of Native South American Indian origin, with the majority of them living in that particular area of the country and the others, mainly of the Mapuche tribe, living in the far south. As is probably true in most countries, these tribal areas were among the poorest of the population, with survival being their main focus.

On his first trip, being totally unaware of what he would find, we outfitted him and the young men who went with him with some canned goods, canned juices, crackers and cookies, and a supply of mate. Fortunately, Mike decided to take his crossbow with him for sporting purposes, thinking it would be a good relaxation method for all of them. The provisions they took were not enough to keep them fed, and they were soon forced to use the cross-bow to hunt for anything they could find that moved. It so happened they shot a stork...and nine months later, on January 2, 1973...the hottest day of that year...our third daughter, Debra Lynelle, was born! (I had been playing the accordion at a river baptismal service the afternoon before her birth – now that was a funny sight! A very pregnant me playing an accordion...picture that!) We always laugh that our Debra truly came via the stork! This time around it was the typical empanadas I craved. One of the other pastors who had been on the trip also became the father of a baby girl around the same time. He previously had three boys. It was determined the stork must have been female!

We also adopted a new puppy just prior to Debra's birth, a very sweet brown dachshund we named Prince. The girls always say he was the only brother they had growing up!

The timing of our new baby's arrival indeed caused a lot of fun and laughter, but that trip was pivotal for Mike – for the rest of his life, his love for the people from that area of Argentina was boundless. He made at least two trips a year to those areas, and those people were a constant source of inspiration to him; ministering to them was one of his greatest fulfillments. It was because of his attachment to them that he acquired a mustache...in their culture, it was a sign that you had entered manhood. He kept his mustache the rest of his life.

On one of his trips a few years later, he was commended by the governor of the province for being the leader of a church that taught faith in such a way that it radically changed and improved the lives of the people. In the governor's speech, he said his people now farmed their lands, sent their children to school, were no longer drunken and treated their wives with respect instead of beating them. Quite a testimony! On one occasion he was granted permission to use the Catholic church to hold the local Foursquare convention in as there were so many people coming, which was probably a once in a life-time event for the Catholic church.

Not too long after Mike's first trip north, I invited Judy Davis to tea. Teatime is almost as much of an institution in Argentina as it is in England. I had made careful preparations, had a lovely table set with my china, and was anxious to honor my friend in the best way possible. She arrived at my home – which could have fit five times over in her home – and we were just getting ready to sit down for tea when the doorbell rang. I went to answer it and found four pastors from that northern area standing at the door. They looked tired, were disheveled and obviously in need of a shower.

I greeted them enthusiastically, but on the inside was completely unnerved…how in the world would I entertain Judy and them at the same time? I introduced Judy to them (she spoke little Spanish) and explained the situation to her. She was ecstatic! So, we moved the tea party outside under a shade tree, brought on the mate elements to join the tea set, added some simple crackers and cheese to the delicate sandwiches and cake, and we all sat around to fellowship. I interpreted as necessary.

After a good two hours, Mike arrived home and Judy forced herself to leave. But she told everyone about that tea party for months, declaring it to be the singularly most delightful cultural experience she had while in Argentina. The northern brothers enjoyed it as well, and I later discovered they had told the people in their churches that Mike was the most humble man they knew...he would come to share and bless them in their simple, rustic settings, yet lived in a house decorated with gold! You see, I had picked up several brass decorative pieces while in Panamá and had them on display as part of my interior decorations. What impressed me most about their perspective was the fact that they did not condemn us for having more, but rather praised Mike for being content to live among them with so much less when it was required of him. There is a deep lesson here somewhere...

On one of his trips to the north for a convention, Mike had just gotten behind the pulpit to preach the evening's message when a young woman ran into the church, up to the platform and handed him a baby. "My baby is dead! Please pray for her!" Indeed, the baby was cold, stiff and its lips were blue. He had no idea what to do but obeyed the Spirit's urging to pray so he lifted the baby heavenward and began praying. After a very short time he felt the baby moving in his arms and returned it to its mother. She took the child, sat on the front bench, and the baby began to nurse. He didn't tell this story often as he felt very humbled to have been a part of it.

****

Early on in my pregnancy with Debra, I traveled to Ecuador with Brenda and Leahna. My brother was going to be there on vacation from college in Ohio, of course my sister was still at home, and my grandmother McCarthy and cousin Carol Yoder decided to join the family for a mini family reunion. It was a great time!

On a Sunday afternoon we all went out in the boon-docks to visit a country church and had to walk over a swinging vine and bamboo bridge to get there. Well, Daddy decided that neither Grandma nor I were going to do that, so we stayed at the car supplied with water and shade trees. We took a little walk, enjoyed seeing some trees and plants, hitherto unknown to us, saw a bit of wildlife, including a turkey hen and some chicks. Upon returning to the car... being pregnant...I needed to find a bush for personal rea-sons. I had just accommodated myself to take care of busi-ness when the turkey hen came running at me in a huff. Evidently she considered me a squatter (literally!) in her domain. Let me just tell you, I moved fast, considering my position and clothing condition! I don't think my Grandma and I ever laughed that hard before or after.

While in Ecuador, we made a day trip to the beach. It was overcast, but obviously warm. We all enjoyed some water fun, I kept the girls shaded, but somehow managed to get the one and only bad sunburn of my life. In fact, it was so bad I was afraid to go to my obstetrician for my monthly check up when I got back to Argentina because I knew he would not be happy with me – and he wasn't!

Our suburb of San Isidro was one of the older parts of the city. Bordered by the River Plate, it was home to "old money," an elite yacht club and golf club, a world-famous horse racing track, historical homes, beautiful modern homes, and everything in between. The tree-lined Avenida Libertador runs through lower San Isidro, and is lined with a myriad of exceptional restaurants, pizza parlors and tea houses. When we had been in Argentina for seven years, the Mission Department finally purchased a home and we made sure it was in San Isidro.

The shopping area, although relatively small, had a well-rounded variety of shops and small boutiques. During our entire twenty years, I did the vast majority of my shopping right there. Whether pushing a pram, stroller, walking with the girls as they grew older, or just strolling along by myself, I never tired of going to our little "downtown" to make a few purchases or to just window shop. In my visits back since we returned to the US, it is one of the things I most look forward to.

One of the first shops I entered upon arriving in Argentina was in San Isidro, a very small narrow shoe store, specializing in children's shoes and bedroom slippers. The owner was a most interesting Jewish lady. She had a brother who owned another shop and a brother-in-law, still another one, all in San Isidro. After having shopped there for three or four years, one day she asked if I knew anyone who taught English, and thus I became a private English teacher to Margot Litchi. The lessons didn't go so well – she will be the first to admit due to the student, not the teacher – but a new friendship was formed and quickly blossomed.

Margot became a family fixture at Thanksgiving and Christmas meals, and I joined her for some of the traditional Israeli holidays. Like so many of my Argentine friends, we still keep in touch and talk by phone from time to time. I can tell you one thing...if you have a Jewish friend, you have a friend for life. Upon her return from one of her trips to Israel to visit her daughter and family, she gave me a small, gold charm, the "Hand of Friendship," a very typical and meaningful piece of Israeli jewelry. I wear it very frequently, always thinking of my special friend, Margot, when I do. When Mike and I were privileged to tour Israel in 1987, she gave me a small, tightly folded piece of paper; it was her prayer request, and she asked me to place it in a crevice at the Wailing Wall in Jerusalem. I did so, and it was a very emotional moment for me.

I have learned that we never know the impact our witness and lifestyle make on others. At Christmas time not long ago, Margot and I spoke by phone during the Hanukkah season. After I wished her a Happy Hanukkah, and she quickly responded with a Merry Christmas to me, she said, "You know, Lolita, Hanukkah is the Festival of Lights. That's why Christ (not only Jesus…but Christ!) was born during that time, because He came to be our light!" I held back my elation, readily agreed with her, and knew her heart was opening to the Messiah. I was completely overwhelmed!

I usually ended my little San Isidro shopping expeditions with a stop at my favorite coffee shop. In the earlier years, there were two or three to pick from, but in the early 80's a new coffee bar opened that became my favorite, "La Bicicleta." My girls all loved it too, and we managed to squeeze in a short interlude there as often as possible. Margot and I met there almost on a daily basis for several years. Wow – I so miss that!

Just prior to crossing the railroad tracks to the main San Isidro shopping street there was a fairly large fruit and vegetable market, open to the sidewalk during business hours. I was walking in that direction and the owner was standing visiting with another guy. As I approached, the owner said to the other guy, as if it were a continuation of their conversation, "That's what I am telling you...if Adam ate an apple for Eve, I would eat this whole market for that woman!" This type of flirting is quite common, and I had to do everything in my might to not break out laughing.

On another occasion I was walking with Debra, around 2 ½ at the time, and a man passed by us exclaiming how beautiful I was. Debra turned around and yelled at him, "Viejo verde estúpido!" (Similar to "stupid dirty old man!") First, I have no idea how she knew the term, and second, I have always wondered whether she thought him stupid for disrespecting her mother or because he said I was beautiful!

Some things you like to forget and are glad when they have become history. Others, well, you don't really miss them, but still have a permanent place in your history. One such item, for me at least, is the old Foursquare uniform for women ministers that was worn in the US for over fifty years and is still worn in many areas around the globe. In Argentina, the uniform consisted of either a white or black dress, depending on the season, worn with a black shield-shaped bib. This accessory was piped in white and at its center held the Foursquare cross symbol. It really was a good thing; many women could not afford nice clothes for the pulpit or platform, but with just one dress for winter and one for summer, they were well dressed and looked sharp.

The only drawback I experienced was that white dresses and small children just were not a good mix. I particularly remember one occasion when I had on my uniform. One of the girls was at the toddler stage...the area we were at was famous for its red dirt...you get the picture. At least

I always made sure to have a spare dress along, and the white ones were always of the wash-and-wear variety, so I was covered – literally and figuratively! Just for the record, I still have a Foursquare shield in my closet. Old habits are hard to break!

The addition of a third little girl to our household made it necessary for us to move to a larger home, and we were so blessed to find just what we needed in the (also northern) suburb of Martinez, right close to San Isidro. It was in this house that I knocked a huge double window off its hinges – with my head – when I bent over to pick something up. I had a pretty bad headache for several hours and black eyes for a few days.

I added an important asset to each house we lived in – clothes lines either in the garage, a hallway or whatever nook or cranny I could find. I did not own a dryer until my youngest child was three. And incidentally, I never had the pleasure of using disposable diapers! In fact, I still did laundry in a wringer washer the early years in Argentina and finally had an automatic washer in 1985. We lived in Martinez for four years, and even though Martinez had a very nice, upscale shopping area, I would consistently find myself hopping on the train and heading to San Isidro!

****

It was around the middle of 1973 that we were overwhelmingly blessed to have my parents move to Argentina as missionaries – not to mention as resident grandparents! They remained in Argentina a total of eight years. They immediately took over the Bible Institutes, traveling to many areas and setting up training centers.

The need for workers and pastors was constantly kept at the forefront, encouraging the youth to prepare for ministry, whether full time or for the day to day ministering to the congregation in their local cities and provinces, and the Bible Institutes, brief institutes and seminars were a great priority. Mike's thought was that if all the students went to Buenos Aires for training, they would begin to settle down there and it would be difficult for them to return to their own areas...so the institute was taken to them. The brief institutes allowed for the teacher to go to the students. There was still the possibility to complete a three-year course for these students even if they were not at an actual institute site.

I traveled as often as possible, as did my parents. Due to the length of some of the trips and Daddy's food issues caused by diabetes, he did not attend the northern events very often. With the girls' school schedules and activities, it was also difficult for me to be gone for the length of time required for those trips. Mommy also organized the women's ministry nationwide and traveled extensively with Mike for that endeavor and was of great assistance to him in the conventions, particularly in the north.

Each year the people would build a new out-house to be used by Mike and the entourage that would go with him. It was a long, two-day trip from Buenos Aires, with an over-night stop at one of the bigger cities. On Mommy's first trip, they finally arrived at their destination. After the greetings were over, she told Mike she needed a bathroom. He told her to ask one of the ladies who would show her the way. Well, the particular lady she asked was unaware of the new out-house and took her to an old one that was hardly standing, had only three walls, and was in quite a bad state. By this time several other ladies had joined the parade. When Mommy saw the condition of the facility, she exclaimed (more to herself than anybody else), "What do I do now?" To which one of the ladies replied, "Anything you want, Sister!" From then on that became a standing phrase in our family…if anyone asks what they should do in whatever circumstance, our pat answer is, "Anything you want, Sister!"

During their absences, Daddy and I would hold the fort on the home front, both at the church we were establishing, as well as keeping up the central office activities. Daddy and I were the home budgeters for our households, and we would give Mike and Mommy their budgeted money whenever they traveled. They were so funny and would constantly think of ways they could save money from their trips to have a little spare stash.

Mommy and Daddy left Argentina in 1981, moving to Mexico where they ministered for four years. Their departure was painful and difficult for all of us. But the impact they made on the Foursquare work in Argentina was immeasurable and is still being felt from generation to generation. They did return for Brenda and Denny's wedding and remained with us a few months following. When they left for furlough and supposed retirement, I took them to the airport to see them off – the last time I was to see my Daddy.

****

Mike was a visionary. Evangelism coupled with training were always purposefully planned to fulfill his vision for raising up both churches and leadership throughout the country. I am more organizational. I planned and scheduled events, put together programming for conventions and seminars, and in general, gave feet to his visions. God knew what he was doing when he put us together! We always worked as a team, and that is one of the greatest blessings I could ever ask for in my own personal ministry.

At different times during our time in Argentina, I served as national treasurer, administrator for the national church office, Bible Institute Director and instructor, head of Women's Ministries, ministered through speaking, singing, teaching, worship leader, counseling, translating, writing educational materials, women's studies and periodicals, TV hostess (with 700 Club) and in so many other capacities. I always ministered along side Mike in all areas, including pastoring, national projects, and church planting. I have never once felt my ministry and ambitions were demeaned or thwarted by him. In fact, he was always my greatest cheerleader, and I truly hope I was the same for him.

The church calendar called for a national convention once a year, which both of us and my parents attended and were completely involved in; the girls also traveled with us for these annual events. Leadership conferences were held at least once a year in some six to eight different locations throughout the country as well as district conventions in each of these places once a year, which included even more training. Pastor retreats were also held at various times and places which added yet another venue of training. Mike attended all of these. When he was gone, the girls and I did all the girlie stuff; but when Daddy was home, we catered to him. In retrospect, I am so glad they made him feel special. His girls were the delight of his life.

During the second convention following our arrival, held in 1972 in the southern province of Neuquén, Mike called the pastors and entire national church to a weekly day of fasting, prayer and intercession for the nation. From then until we left, Wednesdays were set aside for that purpose. And as the political climate worsened, more than ever the church began to sense the urgency of this commitment. We have often been asked, "To what to you attribute the great revival in Argentina?" Our answer is always the same; the consistent, fervent prayers of the faithful. Obviously, many other churches were in prayer as well, but I am forever convinced that the powerful prayers of the Foursquare saints were key to the revival that eventually swept the nation – more about that to come.

· XII ·

Belonging – In Good Times and Bad

*"Life isn't about waiting for the storm to pass.
It's about learning to dance in the rain."*

Argentina has been, shall I say, politically challenged throughout its history, both before and since independence. Following World War II, it had the largest gold deposit in the world, only to have its coffers emptied during the first Perón era. During the twenty years we spent there, we saw a total of eighteen government changes, up to a 4,000 percent inflation rate in one year, and very difficult, austere financial times. We survived the "Dirty War," and the "Malvinas War," (known to most as the Falkland Island War) and many smaller internal conflicts. Each of these etched their particular indelible memories on our minds.

Just briefly…the early months following our arrival were quite possibly the most peaceful, politically speaking. Although there was always tension between politicians, both local and national, things were, on the whole, calm. General Alejandro Lanusse took power through the military in March of 1971, proclaiming his intention to restore constitutional democracy by the end of 1973. His desire was to permit the political parties to be re-established, including the Peronista party that had been banned since Perón's exile.

In November 1972, Perón returned to Argentina for a short visit, the first since his 1955 exile. Subsequently, in the elections of March 1973, the Peronist party would win the elections, with a majority in the legislature. Things began to quickly change and Perón would soon return to Argentina together with his third wife, Isabel Perón. She had been an Argentine dancer who, it is said, he met in a dance hall in Panamá, then married in 1961 in Spain. His first wife died of cancer before he was a known military or political figure. His second wife, Evita, was the power behind his rise to fame. She died of cancer in 1952, being elevated by the lower and middle class to nearly sainthood.

In the early seventies, many staples became more and more difficult to obtain, and homemakers had to resort to various ingenious ways to acquire provisions for their families. Among the items hardest to come by were sugar, cooking oil and – of all things – toilet paper! But my God is a God who supplies ALL our needs, and He did! *"God has been very gracious to me. I have more than enough!"* Genesis 33:11.

At this time we were renting a storage building in the neighborhood of Munro, near San Isidro, where we were holding services for the congregation that had been left "homeless" when Mr. PDP took possession of the church building in the San Isidro area. When Missions purchased a vehicle for my parents, Daddy gave me a Citröen (otherwise known by Mike as a glorified tin can) that he had purchased not too long after arriving in Argentina. As small as it was, I managed to cram up to twelve kids into it to take them to Sunday School at the rented location. And you thought cramming people into VWs and phone booths was a feat!

As only God can arrange, the owner of said building was a wholesaler and one day, upon arriving at the church, he was waiting for us with a 50-kilo (110 pound) bag of sugar. He said it just crossed his mind we might be able to use it and sold it to us at cost! Sugar was no longer a problem. Just a few weeks later, the father of one of the Brenda's classmates, a Colombian businessman who managed the Mazola Products company, delivered a large case of corn oil to our home. No charge – just a gift he thought we could make use of!

And last, but not least...at that time, our home in Martinez was three blocks from the train station. I had gone into the city one afternoon to take care of some money exchanging, dressed up appropriately for downtown trips. When I got off the train in Martinez, I noticed a young man with a gigantic heavy plastic bag filled with rolls of toilet paper. He was selling it and was doing a pretty good business. When I saw him, I literally raced over to him and asked him how much he would sell the whole bag for. While people stood around waiting for me to buy a roll or two, I made a deal for the entire bag, probably some 100 rolls or more! I threw the bag over my shoulder, Santa Claus style, and proceeded to walk the two blocks home through my upper middle class neighborhood, my high heels clicking the whole way. Believe me, I will never forget the look on Mike's face when he opened the front door for me. He turned beet red and said, "Tell me you didn't walk here with that!" But he had no problem making use of my glorious stash!

In the early months of 1973 God led us to a property in San Isidro for the building of the Central Church, National Offices and Central Bible Institute. As we visited the property for the first time, Mike and I both felt strongly it was intended to be ours. We started the process of dealing with the real estate agents and owners, and after much back and forth negotiations, were finally able to purchase it. Mortgages were not an option at that time, and properties had to be paid for within a 90-day time frame. However, through much God-given wisdom, we were able to extend that time to a 120-day time frame and because of the extra time and the fluctuation of the money exchange, saved the Mission several thousand dollars on the transaction.

The property had a long building along one side, pretty much a replica of the first house we had lived in. We knocked out most of the inner walls, leaving a couple small rooms at the back for Sunday school use. We moved from the rented storage building in Munro and used the building on the property as our church during the building process.

Shortly after the purchase, an obviously hard-working Italian gentleman showed up at church. After he had been there a couple of times and learned we were planning to build, he told Mike his son was an architect and would be interested in the project. We had our doubts, but go figure – he brought his son, José Federico, to visit with Mike, and we soon had blueprints and a building project in the works. We could never have asked to work with a more wonderful man! He also did the remodel on the home the Mission purchased in 1978.

Not long after the purchase, we were told an amazing story. A lady who had been a part of the original Foursquare church initiated by Mr. PDP had shared a vision she had during those early years. She told several in the church that the place God intended for the Foursquare Central Church to be built was on a piece of property not too far from where the original congregation met...and yes, it was the property we had just recently purchased!

The building began to go up and people were very impressed by the structure; it is a beautiful church, more of a cathedral, that followed the inspiration Mike had for it. It was filled to capacity on the Sunday it was dedicated, with the beautiful music we had prepared swelling into the high arches of the edifice. *"Oh, give thanks to the Lord, for He is good! For His mercy endures forever."* Psalm 118:1. Again, this will remain in my mind as a monument to Mike's vision for not only the Central Church, but for Foursquare in the country of Argentina.

****

In the matter of Perón and his new wife...for whom the Argentines had little love...there was no middle ground – you were either a Peronista or you were not, and ideologies and tempers peaked. The weeks building up to their return were filled with fiery newspaper and magazine articles, shootings, and murders. The day of their arrival back to Argentina was set for June 20, 1973; the head of the labor unions declared a national strike day so everyone could attend. The people rushed towards Ezeiza International Airport for the big event: men, women, and children; young and old; the strong and the weak; healthy and sickly alike;

faithful followers of Perón as well as the curious; laborers, farmers and students. It holds the record as the largest concentration of people in the entire history of Argentina.

Unfortunately, that day turned into utter chaos, with the different political factions and the national armed forces involved in fracases. By 2:30 in the afternoon the fields near Ezeiza International Airport had become a literal war zone, with bullets whistling through the crowds injuring hundreds and causing a great many casualties.

The plane bringing the Peróns to Argentina was detoured to another landing strip, and the hundreds of thousands who had gathered to welcome him near Ezeiza never had that opportunity. The plane landed at 5:00 p.m., and in the presence of Perón, the Peronist leader, Cámpora, was immediately sworn in as president. Sitting at home watching the events unfold on national television was enough to strike fear in anyone's heart. That night, Perón delivered a brief message broadcast over all national radio and television stations. His purpose was to thank the people from all over the country who had come to welcome him and also to put at rest any fears that he had been injured. By the end of that day, and as night settled in, most of the country's population knew we were in for a rough ride ahead. And we were.

A happy point of that year was the marriage of my brother Gerry to Mary Vyborny. My parents and sister were able to attend the wedding, but I was not. Their union has blessed our family with two daughters.

Shortly after his arrival back to his homeland, on September 23, 1973, Perón was elected president in a special election and at his insistence, his wife, Isabel, became vice-president. Less than eight months later, on July 1, 1974,

Juan Domingo Perón died. leaving his wife as president. (Interestingly enough, Eliana and I were headed into the city by train and were traveling past the presidential mansion just as the announcement of his death was made; he died at the mansion.)

"Isabelita" (as she was called) was knowingly involved with a man in government, a consort who was an astrologist, and between them they proceeded to govern the country by the stars, astrological charts and other mythical, unorthodox means, including witchcraft. As kidnappings escalated and the economy bottomed out, the Argentines' patience wore thin and times were getting more and more tough. Assaults and thievery were on the rise. In general, the country was going to the dogs.

One quiet afternoon during this era I went to take a short nap while baby Debra also slept. Brenda and Leahna had asked to ride their bikes up and down our block, and Mike was sitting in the front room reading, promising he would keep an eye on the girls. I was awakened by loud harsh voices saying, "Get the girls! Get the girls!" I rushed downstairs, asked Mike where the girls were, and he said they were still out riding. We both ran to the front door where we were intercepted by two policeman who told us to get back inside. I screamed at them, asking where my girls were, but they just kept forcefully pushing us back indoors. What seemed like an eternity later, the police returned with our girls in tow.

Evidently our neighbors across the street, who had been on vacation, returned home and saw a van in front of the house loading up all their valuables. Rather than stop, they went straight to the police who came on the scene before the robbers had left. Seeing our girls outside and fearing crossfire, they rushed the girls around the corner to one of their patrol cars until things were under control. That was fine...but it would have been nice if they had told us that when they refused to let us out of the house – it would have saved me losing several days off my longevity!

Bibles were also very hard to come by during this time frame as imports were closed down. One evening a pastor (whom we trusted) came to us with a friend who said he could supply us with five hundred bibles for $500 cash if we could do the transaction immediately. We happened to have the amount on hand that was set aside for another project, so we jumped at the opportunity. Soon the friend, Mike and I headed downtown Buenos Aires on the train, taking a taxi at the Retiro Train Station. The friend gave directions to the cab driver, telling him when and where to turn, and close to a half hour later he told the cab driver to stop. We got out and he told us to wait at the café on the corner while he completed the transaction. He said he would have the bibles on a dolly so we could load them into a taxi and head for home. We had taken enough money with us to also pay for the cab drive all the way home, about fifty dollars.

We ordered coffee and planned how we would best allot the bibles to the different parts of the country. After about a half hour, we ordered another round of coffee and a sandwich to share, becoming somewhat impatient over the long wait. After an hour we became concerned; the area we were in seemed a bit seedy and by then there were few people left on the streets. Nearly two hours after our arrival, we knew we had been "had." And we were also worried about our safety in an area we knew nothing about and given the late hour. We decided to grab a cab back to Retiro and take the train home, where we arrived close to midnight with no bibles and minus $500 cash. *"The Lord himself goes before you and will be with you; He will never leave you nor forsake you. Do not be afraid; do not be discouraged."* Deuteronomy 31:8.

In the summer of 1975, I underwent two unintentional baptisms, thanks to Debra…she loved the water and, whenever we were around a pool, wanted to get in. Twice that summer, while visiting friends for tea, she walked towards the pool – and right on into the deep end. Both times I kicked off my shoes and jumped in after her, fully clothed. No surprise she is now the daughter with the pool! I think when I am really old and decrepit, I will walk into it at the deep end and let her jump in after me!

A truly memorable experience took place in the fall of that same year. Eliana, Debra and I took a trip to minister in Chile. We took the train from Buenos Aires to Mendoza, then a bus trip, then the highlight of the trip…traveling over the Andes Mountains in a narrow gauge train. It was a mixture of awesome, frightening, breath-taking, and marvelous! Incidentally, that train is no longer in existence, deemed too dangerous!

In the early hours of March 24, 1976, there was a military coup, and Isabel Perón was placed under house arrest where she remained for many months until her exile. Others from her government were imprisoned and some simply disappeared. Soon military forces could be seen everywhere, and it became imperative that everyone carry their national identification documents at all times. The law of the day was to imprison first, ask questions later. Communism had made some deep inroads during the few months of the Perón government, and now it was clean-up time.

As with all such internal strife, often the innocent become mixed in with the guilty, and more and more people began to disappear. Add to the mix the fact that now there were paramilitary groups, dressed in what appeared to be regulation military uniforms, and you can begin to imagine the fear that engulfed us all. No one was safe, no one was immune to being taken by one faction or the other, and each time Mike left on a trip I wondered if I would ever see him again. More than once he was stopped and his car thoroughly searched for possible terrorist propaganda. But I kept my concerns to myself and attempted to live in as normal of manner as possible. *"You will keep him in perfect peace, whose mind is stayed on You, because he trusts in You."* Isaiah 26:3. And trust I did!

Martinez was an area where many business owners, large company managers, as well as attaches from the various embassies, resided. We came to a point where we simply stayed awake at night awaiting the sound of a bomb or gunfire, and then tried to settle into sleep. The "Dirty War" was in full swing and the constant kidnappings and assassinations were rampant.

A family whose children attended St. Andrew's School owned a chain of supermarkets. One morning, as they all came out of the house for dad to drive them to school, he was assassinated in front of them. Another family that had been good friends of ours (he was a manager with Phillip Morris) was transferred out of the country due to threats against his life. We frequently went to dinner with them, and the last few times we did so, we were followed by his personal armed guards who then sat at tables close to us in whatever restaurant we dined. A young man from our local church disappeared together with his brother. A fellow missionary of another denomination was held up, beaten, and left by the roadside for dead and his car was stolen. These are just a few of the examples that touched our lives.

A close at hand incident happened when a young man from our church, who was part of the musical team we had, disappeared together with his brother. Many months later one of our men at church said he felt we should call a day of fasting and prayer for Carlos, and we did. The day after that prayer time, our doorbell rang and when I answered it, there stood Carlos! He was many pounds lighter, looked ill, but at least he was safe. His brother was never heard from again.

Traveling home one evening after teaching in the Bible Institute (we were still meeting in Munro at the time), I had a couple of students with me and was going to take them to their bus stop as this would avoid them a lengthy walk on a very cold night. Upon merging onto the Panamerican highway, I was immediately pulled over by uniformed men. They began to question me about anything and everything, wanted me to get out of the car, to which my students replied, "No, the señora does not leave her car. If you want us to get out we will, but she will not." This brought on more interrogations and finally, after nearly forty-five minutes, they told me I could leave but they would follow me home. I immediately decided I would NOT lead them to my home, so I simply drove to the nearest police station and parked the car...they sped up and were out of sight within seconds, probably proof that they were not legitimate officers. I then took the students to the nearest bus stop and went home.

On another evening I had stopped by a barrio near our new church property to drop off a young lady who had been baby-sitting for me. I had no more pulled over to let her out than the car was surrounded by (this time legitimate) soldiers. I had all three of the girls in the car, and of course they were extremely frightened. The girl who I was dropping off was well-known for her fearless, no-nonsense attitude towards life, and jumped out of the car and began to reprimand them for surrounding a proper señora, with children in the car, no less, and they needed to apologize and open their circle and allow me to leave and allow her to go to her house. There were a little stunned by her tirade, but proceeded to do exactly as she had demanded – they apologized to me, saluted my little girls and went out on the street to stop traffic so I could go on my way.

The car of choice for the paramilitary was the white Ford Falcon, which we also drove at that time. I recall an occasion when I had driven downtown, parked the car and went to the offices of our money exchange contact. While there, one of the employees had given me a box of home-grown avocados, so upon going back to the car, I placed the key in the lock of the trunk. As the key rattled around in the lock I wondered why it was already unlocked, but raised it to place the box there. I was shocked to see that the trunk was filled with arms! Scared to death, I gently closed the trunk and then noticed my car parked next to the one I had approached. I shoved the box onto the front seat of my car, backed out of the parking place and took off as quickly as I could. I drove around downtown Buenos Aires for a few minutes, turning on streets here and there to lose anyone who might be following me. I was really shaken and hoped and prayed no one had noticed me. My fear was that I had become a witness to an arms deal and my life would be of little value if either of the parties involved had seen me. I arrived home safely and held my own thanksgiving service!

One would think that the spiritual atmosphere would begin to improve under such frightful circumstances, but people were still proud and thought they would make it through the "Dirty War" through their own efforts and intelligence. But there was more to come...God was not finished with us yet.

It is estimated that some ten thousand people disappeared during the "Dirty War." A side effect of this was the group known as "The Mothers of the Plaza de Mayo." The mothers and grandmothers of those who had disappeared began to band together and make their presence known at the huge plaza in front of the Casa Rosada (Pink House), the seat of government. They wore head kerchiefs, carried placards of their missing children, signs with the projected birth date of an unborn grandchild a daughter had been expecting when she disappeared, and generally kept their cause to the forefront of the government and the entire population. They were, for the most part, somber, quiet and orderly, with occasional eerie candlelight vigils held at the plaza.

Knowing better but not able to resist, one afternoon when I was downtown and knew they were gathering, I went to the plaza to mingle among them. It was a cold day, and although I had no kerchief to wear, I did pull the corner of the poncho I was wearing around my head, simply as a sign of respect for them. I listened to a few of their stories, cried with some of them, and even had the opportunity to pray with a couple of them. My own motherly heart broke with theirs as I imagined the horrible nightmare they were living. My train ride back home was as quiet and somber as their vigils as I pondered what I had heard and seen.

An ugly aftermath of the war that particularly touched these women were the number of military and police officers who were known to have newly adopted babies in their homes during that time frame. Movies have been made about this, and several lawsuits were brought. To this day, the Mothers of the Plaza de Mayo congregate from time to time to remember their lost children and attempt to find unknown grandchildren. Even now, I am filled with sadness when I think of these women from all walks of life whose lives were forever altered by the "Dirty War." Even recently a mass grave from that era was discovered.

A difficult time already, it was made even more difficult by the rising inflation rate. With growing girls, clothing was a challenge. I sewed my girls' clothes all their growing up years, from baby clothes to prom dresses. Sewing was not the problem, but purchasing cloth was. My mother and I chose some of the younger prints from our closets and I took them apart and used them to make dresses for the girls – when all else fails, resort to Yankee ingenuity!

As months went by, it seemed that Generals were put in place by some sort of primitive game of musical chairs. I don't even remember the many changes in heads of the military government that took place during that time, as during that era we had some battles of our own we were fighting. Increasing responsibilities, financial stress, more frequent and longer travels for Mike, exhausting days, lack of rest, all began to take their toll on our marriage. My main goal in those days was to keep my daughters safe from the turmoil our lives were in.

In December of 1977 we left Argentina for a much-needed extended furlough in order to work on our relationship. The girls and I lived with Dwight and Marilyn West in Victorville where I taught in the Assembly of God Christian School during the spring semester of 1977. Nine months after our return stateside, and after much counseling and help from close friends and church leadership, we renewed our vows in the home of Dr. and Mrs. Jack Hayford. Pastor Jack was a great stabilizer for us. His dear wife, Anna, even had a little wedding cake for the occasion. After another five months stateside, we were ready to return to Argentina and pick up where we had left off.

****

In 1978 my sister, Judy, married Alejandro Caceres, a young man from our church. They had three children before leaving Argentina and moving to Oregon in 1991, where they all reside up to the present time.

In the (Argentine) early spring of 1978, with all three of the girls away at school all day, Mike and I sat at our empty table over lunch one day and decided the house was much too quiet and what we needed was another baby! I had already tricked him into another dog...on our recent furlough I had asked him which he would rather have, a new baby or a new puppy. He opted for the puppy, so we shipped a beautiful Sheltie, Lassie, from Oregon to Argentina upon our return from furlough. He became an exceptionally well-trained guard dog.

But now Mike too realized what we really needed was a new baby, and soon we had placed our order. My cravings this time were for strawberries and whipped cream, not a cheap commodity. I will never forget one late evening when the godfather-to-be of the new baby brought me a huge bowl of strawberries and cream...and I ate the whole thing! It was such a sweet thing to do and I know a financial sacrifice as well.

Rebecca Ruth was born on June 30, 1979. (It took us a year to be allowed to legally give her the name her Daddy had chosen, due to Argentina bureaucracy.) I had her at the same hospital, with the same doctor and same room number as I had with Debra. Daughter number four filled the baby void, had a doting mother, proud father, and three older sisters to spoil her rotten...which I am sure they regretted later in life!

On April 2, 1982, yet another political disaster was thrown at the Argentines. In what can only be considered an attempt to cover up the horrible truths that were becoming known about the "Dirty War," the military went into the Malvinas/Falklands and declared their sovereignty. Having been under British domain for many years, the attempt was quickly responded to by Britain and a new war was on. This one claimed the lives of many very young, untrained soldiers. The people were consistently lied to as to the progress on the war; we were all convinced we were "winning."

On the morning following the declaration of war, I was walking to San Isidro, pushing Rebecca in her stroller, chatting to her (in English) as one tends to do with little ones. A couple of very snobbish women crossed the street and were walking behind me. One of them said to the other, in Spanish, "A stinking Brit and her brat! We'll show them!"

I stopped, turned around and in my perfect Spanish said, "No I am not a Brit. And so what if I was? But just so you know, I totally support Argentina, as does my family, including this little innocent child born here!" They made a beeline back across to the other side of the street. Just proves – prejudice is alive and well all over the globe.

Mike had to make a trip to the US at this time for missions-related business, and things escalated while he was gone. I hung the Argentine flag over our front window, and made it known we sided with the Argentines. Before long the USA made known their alignment with Britain. The girls were told by St. Andrew's to no longer wear their uniforms to school, and all things British were now taboo. Unbeknown to me, Brenda carried her back-pack that boldly sported an American flag; she was spat on and made to get off of a public bus on her way home from school one afternoon.

An American family, friends of ours, lived a couple of blocks down on our street. Her husband was also out of the country at this time, so we made a pact with each other...we would remain in Argentina unless one of us decided it was necessary to move our families to a neighboring country for safety. If she decided to go, I would go with her, and vice-versa. We were both pretty strong willed and, in the end, neither of us left. (We were most saddened years later upon receiving a phone call from her on 9/11, telling us that her husband had died when the second terrorist plane hit his office at the Twin Towers. The family of Allen Bondarenko is consistently in our thoughts and prayers.)

During the time Mike was gone, I was in the pulpit

for the Wednesday night service in the San Isidro church. Worship time had just ended and I was about to give the message of the evening. Sitting on the second row, to my right, was a man who had been coming to our church with his wife for a few months, had always seemed cordial enough, and had become somewhat involved in the life of the congregation. As I started my sermon, he suddenly jumped to his feet and began raving about me being another Margaret Thatcher, intent on ruining the country, and on and on.

My girls were there, and I immediately saw some of the ladies run to them and take them out the side door, while at the same time a group of men from the church ran to the platform and surrounded me. Two of our ushers moved to the man and firmly escorted him from the church. To this day I have no idea what suddenly ticked him off, other than the dire circumstance and pressure the population in general was living through. But I will never forget the swiftness with which those dear ladies and gentlemen acted on behalf of my daughters and me. Rather than feel the violence and hatred aimed in my direction by a tool of the enemy, all I felt was the love and concern from God's precious children.

The war continued through the bitter winter months. All of us were knitting or crocheting warm mittens, scarves and caps for the soldier boys and sending them to a designated spot, together with chocolate bars collected by the children; many sent cigarettes as well. What a rude awaking when chocolate bars began to be purchased around the city, containing little notes of encouragement stuck down between the outer wrapper and tinfoil, written to the soldiers from school children!

LOLITA J. FREDERICK-HARRIS

After the loss of many young lives, the destruction of navy ships and military planes and the country in the throes of total economic chaos, the current General came on national television, quite obviously drunk, to announce that we had ceded to Britain. The sense of gloom and doom was almost palpable. The demoralization of an entire nation was a heartbreaking thing to behold. When walking on the sidewalks you felt like you were in a funeral procession. But underneath all the visible disaster the country was living through, God was at work. *"I would have lost heart, unless I had believed that I would see the goodness of the Lord In the land of the living."* Psalm 27:13.

Finally, in 1983 democratic elections were held and Raúl Alfonsín was elected president under the Radical party. President Alfonsín was well liked, governed well for six years, and made great strides in turning the country back towards democracy. On a personal level, we all liked him because he looked so much like an older version of Mike! And as the years passed, Mike resembled him even more. No wonder he was a good president!

By now the nation was in need of greater help than they could supply on their own. Gone was the national pride after having been humiliated by losing a war caused by the whimsy of a military dictator. In its place were the daily findings of mass burial sites, an inflation rate that brought the stock market to its knees, deepening poverty, unprecedented national debt and world-wide ridicule. At last they had reached the bottom and slowly started to realize that God was their only way out.

Before we judge, let us take a look at our own lives. Though we cringe to admit it, we each have the propensity to that same pride that causes us to believe we are invincible – until trouble strikes at our very core. How often have we had to get to our lowest before we looked to the Highest? But there is hope – we too can see Satan fall!

XIII

Revival – At Last!

"I want to live my life in such a way that when my feet hit the floor in the morning, Satan shudders and says, 'Oh no.......she's awake!' "

It was Christmas morning of 1982. We were all in our brief summer pajamas, gathering around the tree to begin the excitement of opening presents, when the doorbell rang. Mike and I both looked at each other, I ran upstairs for a robe and Mike answered the door in his pajama bottoms and tee-shirt. At the curb stood a Rolls Royce, complete with uniformed chauffeur, and at our front door stood a gentleman with what was obviously a bodyguard.

Mike said good morning, and the gentlemen told us he was the former Panamanian ambassador to Bolivia and needed to visit with Mike for a few minutes. Mike excused his dress, explained we were in the middle of Christmas with our children, and welcomed him in. By then I had some decent – if not overly proper – covering on, and we sent the girls upstairs to wait until we had completed our visit. If there is one thing I was always proud about, it was our girls' understanding and respect for our work. On that particular morning there was no fussing or complaints, and they ran upstairs to entertain themselves until our Christmas could continue. Have I mentioned how much I love my girls?

That morning can only be classified as a morning of destiny. Our visitor unfolded his story to us. He was a member of the Foursquare church in Panamá. When his ambassadorship ended in Bolivia, God had called him to go to Argentina and hold campaigns in three areas of the city: the north, the south, and the east. He requested no monetary help of any kind, only suggestions of where he might hold meetings. But most of all, he had come to seek Mike's blessing as head of the Foursquare movement in Argentina. Mike anointed him with oil, and we laid hands on him and prayed that his obedience to the Lord's call would be greatly rewarded. He went on his way and we went back to our family Christmas morning. But that short, simple meeting evolved into the greatest revival Argentina has ever seen.

After the holidays were over, Mike's travel schedule continued. I made it a point to visit one of the revivals being held in one of our Foursquare churches by our Panamanian brother. It was a simple service, he was not an immensely great orator, no great miracles took place that night, but one could feel the Lord's presence. We continued to pray for him as he continued on his mission.

His last campaign was held in the eastern part of the city, a rather rough suburb filled with factories and businesses revolving around the port activities. Again, there were no great visible outward results. However, during one of those nights a young businessman by the name of Carlos Anacondia gave his life to the Lord. God immediately called this man to preach; he had no training, no background, no experience...he was simply a new believer who heard God's voice and obeyed. To say, "The rest is history," would be the understatement of the century. Carlos joined a local church, read and studied his Bible voraciously, in preparation for the call God had placed on his life. God told him he would have five years of ministry to fulfill that call.

****

A personal highlight of 1983 was a trip Mike planned all on his own and surprised me with for our 20th wedding anniversary. We flew to the most northern province of Salta where we saw Cafayate with its red rock canyons, walked through areas of some of the most well preserved colonial architecture in South America, drove past beautiful grape vineyards and dined on the famous empanadas of Salta. We continued on to the province of Jujuy, enjoying a personal tour of the historical cathedral of San Salvador de Jujuy (led by a gentle priest), the famous Quebrada de Humahuaca and the Cerro de los Siete Colores (Hill of Seven Colors), seeing strong remains of the Aymará and Quechua cultures as well as some Inca ruins. On the morning of our anniversary Mike presented me with a beautiful diamond ring; I had lost the diamond from my original rings while washing dishes at the church after a big event. Of course, it saddened me, but I was quite overwhelmed with the new one!

Brenda graduated from St. Andrew's in December 1983, and we had a large birthday/graduation/farewell party for her. I remember two special moments of that time. The first was at her graduation, when the chair of the school board came over to us as we were eating dinner to congratulate us on our wonderful daughter. He said, "Many of us have watched Brenda's life and progress here at school over the past twelve years. We have concluded that, regardless of what many may think or say, it is possible to live a consistent Christian life here at our school and be a strong influence on other students. Brenda has been that. We are now looking into having Bible teachings brought back into the school. This school was originally based on Christian roots from its Presbyterian inception, but somehow, those have fallen by the wayside." We thanked him and told him we would be praying for their direction in that important matter.

The second was at her party. We had invited a rather large number of young people, thinking as one always does that not everyone would attend. Wrong! Not only did everyone we had invited come, but a few unexpected guests as well, who were not close friends, but nevertheless respected Brenda and wanted to honor her by being there. It was quite a party!

We left for an extended furlough a few days following Brenda's graduation. It was a most difficult time for all of us, as Brenda would not be returning to Argentina with us, remaining in the States for college. Remembering her heart break as she said good-bye to life-long friends still brings tears to my eyes. Although our time on furlough was filled with fun and exciting family times, the closer it came to separating our family, the harder it became. A definite highlight of that period was Brenda's engagement to Denny Truett, the son of our long-time friends and missionary contemporaries, Dean and Carlene Truett.

Sometimes it is hard for non-missionary families to understand the intense bond within missionary families. For the most part, the only family they have is each other. Although we were so fortunate to have my parents with us for a lengthy period of our time as missionaries, the girls still had never had aunts (other than Judy), uncles, cousins or other extended family members near. They had each other. They grew up watching out for, defending, and growing closer to each other. They were sisters, but they were also each other's best friends – they still are. And when it came time for us to return to Argentina, I understood in a far deeper way the true meaning of sacrifice.

By the time we returned to Argentina from furlough in mid 1984, there was revival in the air. Within a relative short timespan following his conversion, Carlos Anacondia began preaching in open air meetings. From the onset, these meetings exploded, continuing to grow and grow. He moved throughout various parts of the country, souls came to the Lord by the thousands, people were healed, the demonic oppressed and possessed were freed, and the revival spread like wildfire. The churches who had been praying for a revival were the ones ready to receive and grow the new Christians; those more preoccupied with their own little social circles totally missed out on the growth and the blessings.

We were involved in Brother Anacondia's campaigns in every corner of the nation. I could often be seen at a small, much amplified keyboard playing for the worship time, or singing solos or with our girls. Mike spent many hours in the deliverance tents, praying for the sick and the possessed. The Anacondias were frequent guests in our home and at our local church, so we came to know them well. I believe I have never known a man as humble as Carlos was in those days. He was no doubt the most astounded of anyone at what God was doing through his life. He was the single most God-used vessel to turn the spiritual tide of a nation.

But at this time our family was living through a crisis of our own. Missing Brenda was not just a fact of life; we felt her absence like nothing any of us could have imagined. Our sweet, "nearly" perfect Leahna bordered on the edge of teenage rebellion. Our easy-going Debra Doll had moments of sheer defiance, and our long-since potty-trained Rebecca began wetting her bed. I was (I have to admit) a somewhat hateful basket case, and Mike did his best to deal with us all while working through his own suffering.

During this season, sometime around January 1985, we were participating and ministering in one of the campaigns in Mendoza. When Brother Anacondia made a call for special prayer at the end of the service on one particular evening, my daughter Leahna and I went forward to accompany a young woman friend who needed a touch from God concerning relational circumstances in her life. Carlos would spend as long as it took to pray for people, and often had to be nearly carried out to his vehicle at the end of a long night, due to sheer exhaustion. As he made his way down the long lines of people waiting for prayer, we stood behind our friend as we waited in line. When he reached us, much to our shock, he glanced at her, reached right over her and laid his hands on each of us! We were both slain in the Spirit!

Although a bit confused by the event, I didn't have time to dwell on it until much later that night. We had arrived in the wee hours of the morning back to the pastor's home where we were staying and were eating a late – very late – supper when their phone rang. It was Brenda! Any other time I would have panicked, wondering what could be wrong that she would track us down and call us in Mendoza, some 15 hours from our home. But I was totally calm...and even remained calm when she explained the reason for her call: she had dropped out of college after only one semester, was living with her Grandma Frederick and working as a waitress, and would enroll in L.I.F.E. Bible College the next semester.

As recently as that very day, this would have sent me over the brink into total despair. But I calmly spoke with her, agreed with her decision, she said hi to her Daddy and sisters, and we hung up. Everyone was calm! Amazing! As I tried to relax in bed after a very long day and most of a night, I realized that we had all been teetering on the edge of depression since leaving Brenda in the States. Now I was at total peace! God had used Carlos to intercede on our behalf in the service. I shared that realization with Mike just before we both fell asleep. It took only a few short days for us to realize that the girls too were back to their happy, joyful selves. We continued to miss her but allowed Jesus to carry our weight.

****

Shortly after our return from furlough, I received a call from the headmaster of St. Andrew's asking if I would take on the task of reestablishing a Bible curriculum into the school, to be known as Bible Literature. After much prayer and trepidation, I accepted. I was asked to not only teach but set up the plan of studies for grades two to six and for the freshmen year of high school. I completely enjoyed that time and found myself at school almost as much as at home, between my teaching schedule and the girls' activities!

I hadn't been teaching too long when I was cornered by one of the mothers who said she needed to speak with me. She said they were a strong Catholic family and she was upset because her second grader had told her I was teaching the big bang theory; she wanted her child to be taught the "doctrine of creation," as she called it. I thought a minute, and then could not help laughing...a couple of classes earlier as we studied creation, I said, "And God said, 'Let there be light!' And BANG! There was light!" Well both of us got a laugh out of it, but I was careful from then on how I expressed things!

Class had just let out one morning and in the proper regimented form, my sixth graders were walking by me as they left the classroom. One of the little guys stopped and said to me, "Mrs. Frederick, you are sexy!" I was completely caught off guard but calmly responded, "You don't even know what that means." To which he answered, "Well, that's what my dad said!" I dropped the conversation at that point!

I would often go downtown to the money exchange and then come back to teach an early afternoon class. I was done with both for the day and heading home, taking the shortcut around the back of the school to the train station instead of walking the several blocks around. Unfortunately, I had not been given the notice that there had been several hold-ups along the path. It was a very narrow path, bordered by a high wall on one side and bushy embankment on the other. Walking along (with my hollowed out book full of money) I saw two rough looking guys coming towards me.

They suddenly linked arms, making it impossible for me to pass around them. They kept coming, and I started praying. When they were about six feet in front of me, they both suddenly looked up above and behind me with sheer terror on their faces. They turned around and fled! I looked around and saw nothing, but I am quite sure they must have seen the biggest, baddest angel guarding over me! God's promise was made very real to me that day, *"For He shall give His angels charge over you, to keep you in all your ways."* Psalm 91:11.

I taught at St. Andrew's until we left Argentina, and was privileged to recommend as my successor, my "pseudo" daughter, Florence Zannochi Piazza. I will always be grateful for the opportunity awarded me to have a biblical input into so many young lives.

In those next very short years, Argentina learned the power of a living God. I can't even begin to try to help you envision the sight of hundreds of people being slain in the Spirit when a rather short, unassuming man stood behind a simple revival pulpit and raised his hands in prayer. I could tell you of awesome healings, amazing stories of deliverances, alternative lifestyles being changed, of families being reunited and restored, and of congregations having to embark on immediate building programs to hold the hundreds of people being baptized and joining local churches.

But the revival did not come without great costs. Christians were ridiculed and persecuted; pastors were put in jail; churches were closed by police orders; open-air revival meetings were disrupted by factions from several sides – at times by the police, at times by gangs, and at times by extremist religious authorities. Sadly, many pastors also fell away at that time, caught up in thinking they were invulnerable and filled with prideful imaginations to the extent that the enemy of our soul was given full reign in the hearts and minds. But God's faithful remained firm and His Kingdom continued to grow. The ongoing waves of that era are still felt today in Argentina. And for us, the awesome privilege to have lived and ministered during that time, in that place, is a priceless gift I will never, ever forget.

During this time, I was asked by our dear friend, Mario Bertolini, if I would consider doing some TV shows with him that would be used as add-ons to the half hour 700 Club shows being aired in Argentina. These shows would be based on a co-hosted talk show format, and would include local events, testimonies, and current issues facing the Christians. The 700 Club offices already had 24/7 prayer counselors available by phone, and many beautiful stories came to our attention through this media. After talking with Mike, much prayer and some serious consideration, I agreed to accept the challenge. We would film two or three shows at a time, and they were aired throughout the week.

One day as we were filming, I was sitting on a sofa and Mario was in a chair at an angle from me. We were conversing when suddenly, for no apparent reason, I quickly scooted to the opposite end of the sofa as Mario looked quizzically at me. An instant after I had moved, a huge mounted lighting system that had been hanging just above my head dropped suddenly to where I had been sitting! Truly a miracle, because the weight of it would have caused me great harm at the very least and could quite possibly have killed me. This was only one of several events where we knew the enemy was not happy about our efforts.

Due to my involvement with the 700 Club, we were able to meet and travel with Pat Robertson, his wife and entourage and translate for some of the events when they visited Argentina. This was shortly after the hurricane headed for the PTL Center back in the USA had turned at the last minute and avoided the complex. On one of the flights we took, we interceded for the Lord to hold back a severe storm that would have made it impossible for us to reach our destination in time for the great gathering of pastors who were anticipating Pat's arrival in the province of Córdoba. God intervened and we landed without incident.

Something that still brings me goosebumps when I think about it is an event that happened to one of our young pastors, Juan Fuentes. He was traveling up into the Andes to minister and was involved in a very serious auto accident. He was taken to the nearest hospital and had to undergo immediate surgery to save his arm. The next day the Jewish surgeon who had performed the surgery came to see him and asked him where he was from. The pastor answered and gave him the name of a small city in Argentina where he had grown up. The doctor questioned him some more, and finally asked him, "Where did you learn to speak such perfect Hebrew?" The pastor was very perplexed, and said, "I don't speak Hebrew." The surgeon said, "Oh yes you do...you spoke to me in Hebrew about Jesus the Messiah the whole time you were under anesthesia!" Wow! That just rocks my world every time I think about it.

I thoroughly enjoyed the time I was granted with the 700 Club and the people I was able to meet and interact with. We filmed around one hundred shows over the several months of the project. The only downside was the need to always look my best when I left the house – I was now a recognized "somebody," even being asked for my autograph from time to time!

During the (Argentine) spring of 1984 I flew to Chile to record a cassette with the Trio Ebenezer working with me on the instrumentals and back-up voices. (I had made a small two-sided record a few years prior to help raise money for the building fund of the central church.) The recording sessions went smoothly and quickly, and soon I had five hundred cassettes to take back to Argentina. Another five hundred would be delivered to me, at a later date, by a truck driver who traveled between Santiago, Chile and Buenos Aires. I had purchased the plastic cases and had the paper inserts done at home before I recorded, as that part of the project was less expensive there. I packed the cassettes between clothing in two suitcases, in my carry-on and my large handbag.

The closer we got to landing in Buenos Aires, the more concerned I became about how I would get all those cassettes through customs; I began praying for wisdom as we started our descent. I suddenly started feeling very ill, with a massive headache, dizziness and weakness. The more I prayed, the worse I felt. Upon landing one of the flight attendants assisted me off the plane. I cleared immigrations and the officer, who could obviously tell I was quite sick, brought a chair and told me to sit down while he got the customs officer. That officer loaded my luggage onto a cart and asked if anyone was there to meet me. I gave him Mike's name, he walked out to the area where people waited for their travelers and located Mike.

Leaning on Mike as he pushed the luggage cart, we made our way to the main exit – without any of my suitcases being opened for inspection! The closer we got to the exit, the less ill I felt, feeling totally fine by the time we reached our car. I had often seen the power of God in healing people, but never had thought He would use His mysterious ways to get me through customs! The profit from the sales of those cassettes was used to help finance many needs as the work continued to grow.

July 1985 brought us a great event...Brenda and Denny Truett were married! They had a small US ceremony in their pastor's office in Monterey Park, California, after which Brenda traveled immediately to Buenos Aires to prepare for the real event that would take place two weeks later on July 6th in her home church. And what an event it was! Our family was increasing and we were all thrilled. Denny's parents were there, one of our cousins came, and my parents returned to Argentina for the big day as well.

My parents stayed on for a few months following the wedding, for what ended up being a great gift from God. I will always remember my birthday on May 5, 1986, when my sweet Daddy picked roses from his garden and brought them to me at breakfast time with a little bag of fresh sweet rolls so we could have our coffee together. In August of 1986, they returned to the States to retire, visiting several countries where they had ministered during their time as missionaries. When they arrived in the States, they were asked to return to Honduras as semi-retired missionaries, just to be an encouragement as the work had traversed some difficult waters. They agreed to do so.

I had just completed a speaking engagement at a women's conference in Santiago, Chile on October 21, 1986, and would be flying back home on the afternoon of the 22nd. On that morning I received a call from our former mission's director that changed our family forever. My sweet Daddy had simply gone to sleep and awakened in heaven in the early hours of the 22nd. He and Mommy were to have taken a plane to Honduras on that day, and he had made mention to Mommy that this was one trip he didn't want to miss – and he didn't! I flew from Santiago, Chile to Ezeiza International airport where Mike met me with a suitcase of items I had requested, then flew straight to Los Angeles.

The next month is a mixture of so many visiting us at the missionary home, the funeral, helping Mommy settle Daddy's affairs, and finally taking her to Honduras. She wanted more than anything to fulfill the assignment they had accepted, and she knew that was what Daddy would want her to do. On the final day I was in Honduras with her, their shipment – that Daddy had packed – arrived, and I had to go through everything and take care of dispersing of Daddy's personal items that Mommy did not want to keep.

By the time I arrived back home to Argentina, I was exhausted mentally, physically and emotionally. I finally came face to face with my own personal grief. It is in those weakest moments that God comes in like a rushing river and restores us, lifts us up on wings of eagles, and renews our strength beyond comprehension. During that time I learned more than ever, that the joy of the Lord is my strength. *"But those who wait upon the Lord shall renew their strength; They shall mount up with wings like eagles. They shall run and not be weary, they shall walk and not faint."* Isaiah 40:31.

****

Around late 1987, the Lord began to speak to Mike regarding our leaving Argentina. He felt impressed that we had accomplished what the Lord had sent us to do. During the years he had served as supervisor of the Foursquare Church in Argentina, the work grew from some thirty churches and meeting places to over seven hundred. During this time over 260,000 souls were won to the Lord, hundreds of ministers and lay pastors had been trained, youth programs and camping layouts had been established as well as children's ministries, women's ministries, Bible training and institutes. The work had been registered as the Foursquare Church in Argentina with all the proper government authorities in the country, and a strong indigenous church had been built.

He had no argument with the Lord; his only "however," was the fact that God would have to tell me personally, because he was not about to do so! My personal agenda was to remain in Argentina until I died. We often joked about him retiring in the mountains of Colorado, me on the beach in Argentina...we would visit on weekends!

The year 1987 brought us another wonderful blessing – Brenda and Denny were appointed as missionaries to Argentina, to work in Mendoza with the Bible Institute. The city of Mendoza had been particularly touched by the ministry of Carlos Anacondia, and the Foursquare churches in the area had grown by leaps and bounds. The training and preparing of new pastors for the fast-growing work was imperative, and Brenda and Denny stepped up to the plate.

The greatest thrill was when they stepped off the airplane with Brenda wearing a cute tee-shirt stating, "Baby on Board!" I became a grandma at that very instant! Audra Michelle was born in Mendoza on April 20, 1988, and I was right there to help welcome her. Leahna made all the flight arrangements for Debra, Rebecca and her to fly in on Friday when school was out. They were all three very proud aunts! Mike arrived shortly after and spent a week enjoying his new status of Grandfather. It was Michelle who started calling him "Papu," and he has been Papu to all his grandchildren (twelve grandchildren, two grandchildren-in-law and four great grandchildren at this point!) from then on. We later learned that "Papu" meant Grandpa in Greek...a token of the intelligence of our grandkids!

****

One of my responsibilities was to take care of exchanging the dollars we received into our local currency, both our personal living funds as well as funds designated for different projects throughout the country. I was able to make the exchange from the personal home of my agent a few times, but that became a danger for him as the word would get out that he kept large sums of money in his home and he would be broken into and robbed...this happened to a couple of agents I dealt with. The norm became for me to go downtown and exchange the money where the agent had an office at a travel agency. I carried a book I had cut out an indention in to carry the cash, and I would leave the travel agency with either a travel brochure or a (empty) ticket envelope, visible to all.

It was a particularly hot summer day; upon leaving the travel agency I decided to take a cab to the train station to return home, even though I usually walked to the station – but it was just too hot. I jumped in a cab at the corner. The first thing I noticed was the driver was a bit scruffy looking, wearing a t-shirt instead of the white or blue shirt and tie required of the drivers. But given the heat, I didn't pay much attention. He asked me where I was going, I told him, and we started out. As we proceeded, he asked what train I took, and I said it was the one to San Isidro. As we approached the station, he did not go towards the curb where he should let me out, but rather stayed in the middle lane of the avenue. I told him I needed out; he chuckled and said he would just take me all the way to San Isidro, a good forty-five minute drive. I said I could not pay for that and he said we would figure it out. Now I was frightened and suddenly noticed that he looked nothing like the picture on the plastic identification sheet hanging over his seat for passengers to see.

I slowly eased my arm towards the door handle, thinking I could jump out in the middle of the traffic and hopefully get away without being run over. He gruffly told me to not even think about it. As I silently prayed, I felt impressed to just talk a blue streak...so I did. I started telling him about our church, the travels we had done throughout the country, the subjects we taught in our Bible Institutes, that I would soon be a grandma, and on and on. He kept saying, "Why can't you just be quiet?"

We were nearing Palermo Park area and he suddenly turned in there. The park is immense, with multiple little side roads one can easily get lost in. Now I was really concerned; up until then I figured it was money he was after, but when I questioned him as to why we were going into the park, he responded with, "Come on, don't tell me you don't have time for a little -------- on such a pretty day! And you won't have to worry about paying either." I began praying in the Spirit – out loud – and he sort of freaked out.

The park was so full that day, no private spots anywhere, and cussing, he turned out of the park, back onto the main avenue and again headed toward San Isidro.

We finally entered the one-way street paralleling the train tracks in San Isidro where the local taxi cabs parked to await fares. I knew most all the drivers as we used their services constantly. He was forced to stop as crowds were crossing the street that had just exited the train. I grabbed the opportunity, jumped out of the cab and darted to the local cab at the front of the line. I was crying and told a driver, one who I knew quite well, that the city driver had practically kidnapped me and please, just get me home. The driver turned and yelled at his co-workers to keep the city cab penned in so he could not follow us, which they quickly did. The man was now standing in the street yelling that I had refused to pay him; the local two or three cabs just idled their engines in front of him, denying him exit.

When we finally pulled up at my front door, I was near hysteria. The cab driver helped me out and into my gate. I rang the doorbell and as Mike opened the door, I turned to pay the driver. He insisted we would take care of it another time, to go inside and calm my nerves. That took a while! Again, I was so aware of God's protection and we were all grateful for my safety. Maybe this is a good place to reiterate the fact that I come by my grey hairs naturally! *"The Lord Himself will fight for you. Just stay calm."* Exodus 14:14.

It was within the next few months that I sensed that our life would be changing. One day as Mike and I were relaxing over a glass of iced tea, I said, "We are not going to be here forever, are we?" He looked over at me, and quietly responded, "No, honey, we aren't."

That was probably one of the most ominous moments in my life. The past couple of years had held many changes, and I knew I would be taking Leahna to the States in August of that year for college. My life as I had known and planned it was coming to an end.

Sitting in my favorite coffee shop a few months later, I was really feeling blue, sorry for myself and dismally sad by the thought of leaving my adopted homeland. Just the thought of packing up our home and saying farewell to so many loved ones caused me to tear up ever more frequently. On this particular early fall morning, there was a steady drizzle and the thought of good hot coffee urged me on. I sat at a corner table, ensconced between the little beveled windows that added such charm to the place. I ordered my coffee and after it was served, I sat there gloomily staring down into the cup. Suddenly I did a double take and looked more intently into my cup...there on top of my coffee was a small rainbow! The sun was trying to peek through the clouds, and as a ray made its way through the beveled glass, it formed the miniscule rainbow in my coffee cup!

It was a special moment...I was reminded how the Son shines through our tears and brings us hope in the midst of despair, joy in the sadness and courage to move forward despite the circumstances that may surround us. Just the memory of that instant always fills me with awe and wonder. His loving care and concern for each of us individually is unequaled!

June 22, 1988, marked our twenty-fifth Wedding Anniversary. I decided we would celebrate big time, and planned quite a party, with the renewing of our vows officiated by Denny, my daughters singing, a beautiful reception, and lots of friends to help us rejoice. It was a lot of fun, held deep meaning for us, and marked an important milestone in our lives together.

Leahna graduated from St. Andrew's in December 1987 and stayed with us until August 1988 when she and I traveled to Ada, Oklahoma to leave her in the home of our very dear friends, Marilyn and Dwight West. They had graciously opened their arms, their hearts and their home to Leahna, and she was soon enrolled in East Central University. Although the West's son, Don, was not aware of it at that time, Leahna had told me when she was fifteen that she would be marrying him...and that he didn't need to know it yet!

I took a while for Don to figure it out, and our whole family went to Ada for the beautiful wedding of Leahna and Don West on May 19, 1990. The Monday after the wedding, my mother traveled back to Argentina with Debra and Rebecca, staying with them for a month while I had surgery and recuperated. Mike stayed with me in Ada, and it was a time of soul searching and decision making for both of us as we anticipated what the future held for us.

XIV

Don't Cry for Me, Argentina

"Sorrow looks back, worry looks around, and faith looks up."

During the month spent in Ada, we spoke with the Foursquare District Supervisor who offered us the pastorate of a church there upon our permanent return. The denomination had just purchased a small, old church building, but it did not have a pastor. The small congregation had dwindled to near nothing. We had also been offered a couple of major things out in California, which we knew were not right for us; so we told Dr. Westbrook that if the church was still without a pastor upon our return, we would consider that as a sign from the Lord to us, and take the church.

The months leading up to our departure flew by all too quickly. It wasn't until Mike's fiftieth birthday was just around the corner that I really came to grips with the whole moving issue. I teeter-tottered back and forth between mild anticipation and total despair. I had trouble facing the fact that my Daddy had "died in the missionary saddle," and my mother was still in Honduras (although she finally retired in 1990). Here I was, still relatively young, leaving the field. I knew it was what God had impressed upon us, but even that made no difference to my rebellious mind! I felt like I was somehow betraying my parents, not to mention my own broken heart at thinking about leaving my beloved Argentina. I know that sounds crazy, and I knew then that I was being selfish, that I needed to make things easier for everybody by having an attitude adjustment, but sometimes it just seemed impossible.

The week prior to Mike's birthday, I was sitting at church following our weekly afternoon women's meeting. The ladies were planning all the salads they were going to prepare for Mike's big birthday bash asado, and not wanting to influence them, I was leafing through my Bible, lost in my own little world. I glanced down at a particular page and noticed some of the letters seemed much darker than others. Having had some difficulties with my eyes, I chalked it up to that and made a note to self that making an appointment with an optometrist would need to be one of the first things I did when back in the States. I leafed through pages another time, and again noticed dark letters. Only this time, I realized it was the same passage that I had opened to before.

Now curious, I started reading...Leviticus 25:10... *"And you shall consecrate the fiftieth year, and proclaim liberty throughout the land to all of its inhabitants. It shall be a Jubilee for you; and each of you shall return to his possessions, and each of you shall return to his family."* It was like a knock up-side my head! Here we were planning Mike's fiftieth birthday – his year of jubilee – and the Lord was telling me in very plain words that it is time for Mike to return to his own possessions (land) and to his own family! I won't say I liked it, but at least it released me from the torture I had been putting myself through. And so it was that on August 7, 1990, as we celebrated with so many family and friends, I finally came to grips with reality. It didn't make it any easier in the natural, but I had settled it in my heart and my spirit.

We did not make public our plans until three months prior to our moving date. Once we did, our phone rang constantly, people wanting to talk to us, to cry, to take us to dinner, have us to their home for an asado, to ask why we had to leave. Our home was an on-going open house as people traveled from different areas of the country to say their good-byes. We started selling personal items, giving things away, boxing up things to pack. Those days are not among my happiest memories.

On November 10, 1990, the truck carrying the sea container that would contain, store, and eventually ship our belongings, arrived at our front door. Throughout the day we controlled, organized, and watched as everything was packed in the huge container. I had carefully packed all our family and other personal pictures in a huge trunk to take with us on the plane, but at the last minute had it included in the shipment. Debra and Rebecca were at school that day, so they did not have to watch the painful agony the process caused both Mike and me. By they time they came home that evening it was all over and done with, the container was gone.

I have no way of explaining the enormous tsunami wave of sadness that swept over me as I watched that truck pull away from my beloved home. The law at that time was that when, as a permanent resident you left Argentina, anything you wanted shipped abroad had to stay in storage for a minimum of six months, possibly a year, before the government would release it. At the very least, it would be over six months before we could set up home again, and most likely as long as a year. My insides literally twisted as all that meant home was taken from me. In that moment of desperation, I quietly prayed, "Please Lord, six months…let it be just six months!"

In the last month we attended many farewell parties. I cried daily as I said good-bye to yet another friend, I walked to San Isidro every single day just to breath in the air. I took train and subway rides to various areas in our northern suburbs and to the city, just to spend one last moment there. I don't know if Mike was aware of all I was going through, but he certainly was aware of constant tears. (OK – so now I have to stop and mop up…I am crying even now!) Remember, we were also having to say good-bye to Brenda, Denny and our grandbaby, Michelle. They had moved to Buenos Aires by this time and were taking up residence in "our" home; they would now be working out of Buenos Aires and pastoring the San Isidro church.

Getting through the second weekend in December 1990, was quite a feat. Debra graduated from high school at St. Andrew's on December 7th and said good-bye to all her friends and classmates; I said good-bye to co-workers, and we all said our good-byes to teachers and parents. That Sunday, December 9th, was our last service in San Isidro, followed by a dinner. My tears were non-stop and even I was upset with me for not being able to stop the flow. By the time the last hug was given and the last cheek kissed, we were all completely drained. We went home to spend our final night there. We all cried ourselves to sleep.

The following morning the last items were placed in suitcases, our dog, Laddie, was finally put in his travel cage, and by mid afternoon we were on our way to the airport. We had requested that only the drivers of the vehicles taking us and our luggage go to the airport, but many others still showed up. By then we just wanted to get on the plane and be done with it...and that moment came all too quickly. I have visited Argentina a few times since then, and I will admit I cry all over again each time I land, and each time I take off. That's just the way it is.

Stories about those twenty years in Argentina could go on and on...showering in the back yard under pouring rain after a drought; deep health concerns when one of the girls became ill; Mike's battle and healing from vocal cord nodules; my diagnosis with arthritis at thirty, when the doctor told me I would no doubt be using a cane by forty, walker by fifty and wheel chair by sixty...but God!

I could tell about young man who fell over twenty-five feet from a ladder to the concrete floor while changing a light bulb in our church's breezeway; we prayed over him while waiting for the ambulance and he was in church the next day, sore but perfectly well. Then there's the time a young man who had severe mental lapses came to the house with a gun to settle "a score" with Mike...again, God intervened.

Beautiful memories of visiting homes throughout the country – homes of every class of people – and enjoying them all midst titillating conversations; people healed of cancer; helping pastors' wives learn to make the most of their meager wardrobe funds; giving etiquette classes to young girls; sewing wedding dresses, making wedding cakes and giving young couples the best wedding possible; getting caught in a flash flood on a bitter cold morning in my Renault and having to push it out by myself…I had on a pair of jeans and when I got home, my mother was with the girls. She told me to immediately take off my wet clothes at the heater by the front door, so I did. Then she was horrified because I was turning blue, but actually the jeans had faded on my legs!

Cooking for up to hundred people out of my very small kitchen; last minute meal shopping and preparation for five hundred people at a convention when the groceries were not delivered as promised – this on an outdoor temporary cook site! Housing 30 women in our home at an early convention by means of wall to wall mattresses.

Trotting on horse-back along the beautiful foothills of the Andes mountains with sheep wandering about, standing in awe at the foot of the freedom monument at Cerro de la Gloria in Mendoza, coffee moments at a myriad of quaint little coffee bars, Sunday afternoon strolls though the local park at the arts and craft fair, enjoying world renowned exhibits at museums and sitting in the well-manicured gardens of friends for a pleasant afternoon teatime. Getting to visit in the home of famous painter, Lola Frexas (arguably Argentina's most important watercolorist), who presented me with one of her works after our tea time; together with Mike and our girls meeting author Jorge Luis Borges, a key figure in Spanish and universal literature; attending classes under Leo Tavella, famed Argentine ceramist and sculptor.

Yes, I could go on and on. I have many amazing memories to draw from those twenty years. To this day, when I want to settle my mind in a quiet place or memory, it is to Argentina that my mind returns. They were without a doubt the best years of my life as I raised my beautiful daughters (have you become aware of how much they mean to me?), ministered together with Mike in the country of my calling and lived in the land of my heart. But God always has more...

· XV ·

Rough Landing

"I've learned that instead of viewing God's love through my circumstances, I need to learn to view my circumstances through His love."

We landed in Oklahoma City, Oklahoma, on December 11, 1990 – almost twenty years to the day that we landed in Buenos Aires, Argentina for the first time. Leahna, Don, Marilyn, Dwight and a young man Debra had been corresponding with all met us with their various vehicles to transport our twelve suitcases, eight handbags and one dog to Ada, Oklahoma. We were once again starting over; it's one thing to do that at twenty-five and thirty, another thing altogether at forty-five and fifty!

During the nearly seven months since our last time in Ada, several pastors had taken an interest in the church, but it never worked out. One couple actually pulled into town with their moving van, spent a weekend, and kept right on going. So it was that we had accepted the pastorate, setting the first Sunday in February as the date we would become pastors. We felt we needed those six weeks to get our feet on the ground. In the meantime, ministers would come each Sunday to fill the pulpit.

We had never owned a home or furniture (other than little accent pieces), and had not owned our own car in nearly twenty-five years except for a couple of cars I had for a time in Argentina; we had no idea about health insurance, US taxes, medical costs, the school system, etc., etc., etc. For some twenty-five years, most things had been taken care of for us by our Mission Board. We never had much money, but we were always well provided for. Now it would be all up to us. But even though we were leaving our home in Argentina behind, we were excited about these yet again new beginnings and knew we were where God wanted us.

We moved in with Marilyn and Dwight; they had five bedrooms with baths, and all their kids were married and out of the house, so it was a good arrangement. The house was to the east of town on ranch property. Our plans were to stay with them until we either bought a home or built one. In the meantime, we began to purchase bedroom furniture for ourselves and for each of the girls...those married West kids had taken theirs with them! I also started buying bedding and kitchen things, such as new dishes, flatware and small appliances. I enjoyed the shopping, even though sometimes I would have to just leave the store in the middle of a shopping spree and go back home, overwhelmed by the enormous variety of things available.

I offered to do the main cooking for us at Marilyn and Dwight's. I was not working, I loved to cook, and we all loved to eat, so it was a great deal! Again, grocery shopping was quite an ordeal for me...too many choices, products I knew nothing about, and products that I was used to that were now no longer available to me. More than once I left the grocery store in tears, stressed and confused from all the products to choose from. I had cooked from scratch all my life, and even after some thirty years still have not learned to take advantage of all the ready-made items or all the canned and frozen goods that could make my cooking so much easier!

And so, we settled in. We enrolled Rebecca in the middle of sixth grade. She had already completed sixth grade at the top of her class at St. Andrew's but she was by far the youngest in her class and we did not want to push her into junior high and the middle of seventh grade, knowing her culture shock would be difficult enough with adding pressure of entering junior high. We made a wise choice.

Debra decided to wait and enroll at East Central University the following fall and found a part-time job at Payless Shoes, and also cleaned some houses, so she could get herself on the right road financially. I planned to wait two or three months before entering the work force and attempt to find a job. In the meantime, we needed to purchase a vehicle, and we did – a very old, very well used vehicle, for $1,000. But it worked until we were more stable and ready to move up a few notches.

At the early part of February, Brenda and Michelle came to Ada to await the birth of a second child. We were all convinced it was a boy, and if born in Argentina he would have to do military service at eighteen or never be able to return to Argentina without paying a huge fine. Also, they really wanted to give him an English family name. Denny arrived in Ada on February 12th, and Justin Dean arrived on February 14th – a BOY – which none of us, mom, grandma or aunts, knew what to do with in our all girlie family! But we were thrilled and figured it all out pretty quick.

During the week of February 22, 1991, Mike flew to California to visit his mother. I covered at the church and all was well. On Monday morning Rebecca left for school; Brenda, Denny and their two little ones, Michelle and Justin, as well as Debra, were all at "home," meaning Marilyn and Dwight's. I went into town to take donuts and to pray for an elderly couple that had trouble getting out for church. After that I looked at a couple of houses that were for sale by owner, then headed back east out of town to the ranch.

As I neared our road off the highway, I saw a fire truck pull away from a fire hydrant on the highway, then turn down our road. I saw billows of smoke and wondered if the fields had caught fire. As I neared the house, I realized that was what was burning! I hurried down the road and passed Debra's bike left to the side. I pulled into the driveway, and all I saw was the house in flames Denny holding his head with his hands, fire trucks, an ambulance, and a TV van. In that instant I know I lost ten years off my life. I saw no one else...no other family members.

I jumped out of the car screaming Denny's name; he came and grabbed me and assured me everyone was OK, they had all escaped with their lives, even our Sheltie dog. Debra had been the first to discover the fire, alerted everyone, they tried to call 911, but the line was already burnt. Debra raced on her bike to the nearest neighbor (in her pajamas and robe) but could not make it so jumped off the bike and ran. The neighbor had already seen the smoke and dialed 911 before she got there, then they went to pick up Brenda and the babies.

The house was a total loss, as were all the contents. Insurance coverage was not nearly enough to cover all of the Wests' things plus ours. All our clothes, jewelry, Mike's fiftieth birthday treasure, special keepsakes we had brought with us from Argentina, all my journals (reason for uncertainties in exact dates for various events in this writing) and a book which I had started, new furniture and household items were all gone, as well as Leahna and Don's wedding pictures and her beautiful dress...but we were all safe. I have never looked at or thought about "things" the same since that day. They are, in the end, just things, and not all that important.

That night we stayed with various families, eventually moving in with Glenn and Roberta Harris (Marilyn's parents), taking up residence in their basement. It turned out to be a good thing, because a couple of weeks later we had a close call with our first tornado. Oklahoma was giving us its best welcome! We strongly felt all this was a direct attack from the enemy and determined not to let it discourage us. *"Wait on the Lord. Be of good courage, and He shall strengthen your heart. Wait, I say, on the Lord."* Psalm 27:14.

During that time, we quickly became aware of the giving, caring spirit of the people of Ada. So many things were given to help us all immediately after the fire, and even Rebecca's school teachers thought of the little things that would give her some comfort at losing all she had. Our great Foursquare family from all over the USA sent help, replacing Bibles, bedding, cash donations, and so much more. We were overwhelmed by all the generosity.

****

I started working for Home Federal Savings and Loan the first of April 1991, at first part-time, then full-time. By then we decided not to even consider building a house, but rather to purchase. A house we had seen almost a year earlier when we had come to the States for Leahna's wedding had been taken off the market, and now was on again. Through a series of small and large miracles, we were able to purchase it!

We had little to move…clothes that had been given to us, a few kitchen and household items, that was about all. We repurchased furniture; a family owned furniture store in town, where we had already bought furniture once, replaced it for us at cost. We bought an inexpensive front room set, and I had bargained with the people we bought the house from to leave the dining room furniture, the dinette set, refrigerator and microwave. On move-in day, the furniture store delivered all the furniture, we moved the small items, and in just a few hours we were in our own home! That first evening we sat out on the back patio and watched as a white dove came and perched on our roof; it remained there for the next three days and I always considered that a sign of blessing.

Now, here is the amazing "rest of the story." Remember, I told you that on the day our house was packed up in Argentina I had prayed, "Please Lord, six months… let it be just six months!" I did not want to live in limbo, but so desired to settle into a place of our own within six months rather than maybe as long as a year. Well, I prayed that prayer on November 10, 1990; we moved into our new home on May 10, 1991! And within just a very few weeks, our shipment arrived and we had everything under one roof. God is so absolutely awesome!

From the first Sunday at our new pastorate, when sixteen people were present for that first service, the church began to grow and prosper. (Of course, that first Sunday included us, Leahna and Don, Debra and Rebecca!) The church soon adopted the name of Victory Life Fellowship, and their motto was – and still is – "Where love abounds." Within a short time, Glenn and Roberta Harris and Melvin and Charlotte Harris came back to their Foursquare roots after having spent several years in an Assembly of God church. Other Harris and West family members began attending along with many new people, and the church grew. And our own family grew when Debra married Terry Truett on June 19, 1993, a very happy event for all of us.

Before too long, Glenn and Roberta donated an acreage east of town for a new building and plans began along with fund raising to begin the building of our new church home. Excitement ran high, we were kept very busy and the congregation continued to prosper. By then I had added a second part-time job to my plate, teaching a few Spanish classes at the local university from time to time. Mike was spending his summer months cutting hay for Dwight. Life was moving along full blast.

On Wednesday, August 30, 1995, Marilyn and Dwight were traveling to Branson, Missouri to set up things for a wonderful family get-away we all had planned for Labor Day weekend. They had stopped by our little church early that afternoon on their way out of town to say good-bye to Mike. He said they were so happy and excited about the upcoming weekend. About half-way though their trip, a drunken semi truck driver crossed over the median, hitting their car straight on; they both died instantly.

We were the first to receive the news, as the police called our home that Wednesday night right after we got home from church; they had found a church bulletin in the car with our numbers on it, and no other phone numbers were found. The next few hours were a blur as we gathered their children together and told them, then went to notify Marilyn's parents, her brother, Dwight's brother and mother.

The impact of that loss was felt not only by the family and church, but the entire city of Ada was affected. I tried so hard to be strong for everyone...their children and grand-children, their parents and siblings, our church family, our children, Mike...it wasn't until some three months later that I got up on a Saturday morning and simply fell apart. I final-ly allowed myself to grieve. Marilyn and Dwight had been so dear to us, Marilyn was my sister, more than a friend; the three of us had graduated from high school together, shared so many fun times – and some rough ones as well. Their seemingly untimely home-going has probably been the most difficult thing I have had to come to terms with. A verse I clung to during that difficult time was, *"Fear not, for I am with you. Be not dismayed, for I am your God. I will strength-en you. Yes, I will help you. I will uphold you with my righteous right hand."* Isaiah 41:10.

Marilyn had started a counseling ministry through our church, and Dwight was heading up a recently formed building committee for the church that was being planned; funds for building had already began to grow. The void they left in so many areas was too difficult to even grasp. But the Lord was still on the throne! A multi-purpose building was built at Tipton Terrace and was dedicated November 15, 1998 with very little indebtedness.

The early years were painful as we and the congregation went through some very difficult times; not only did we bid farewell to Marilyn and Dwight, but other key members of the congregation, Dr. Bob Garner and Leon Wade, went on to their eternal reward. Yet God was faithful and the church family grew stronger in their bond of love as well as in numbers.

****

Between August 1995 and July 1996, we were blessed with three more grandchildren: Heather Nicolle, August 5, 1995 (to Brenda and Denny) in Glendale, California; Dylan Dwight, December 26, 1995 (to Leahna and Don) in Ada, Oklahoma; and Kendra Lynelle, July 8, 1996 (to Debra and Terry) in Brownwood, Texas. This grandma had a lot of traveling to do to keep up with that!

I stayed with the bank for six years, then worked at Ada Sales and Rental, then owned by Melvin Harris. After several months there, I worked at the church office. However, with medical costs rising and insurance having to be paid by the church, I felt I could better serve the congregation by re-entering the public work force and became a part of Pre-Paid Legal Services, Inc. on January 10, 2001. In August of that year I started teaching Beginning Spanish at East Central University, first for two noon hours a week, then two evenings a week. I also started doing free-lance translating for several medical and legal entities in town. I was very blessed – my boss at Pre-Paid Legal Services, Inc. was Kathy Pinson, who was not only our church treasurer and secretary who continues to keep the church financially well grounded, but also a dear friend and sister in Christ. I still miss working for her.

On October 7, 1998, we received a double blessing with the arrival of Brittany Leanne and Tiffany Breanne, twin daughters of Leahna and Don, born in Ada. And a few months later, on April 17, 1999, Alan Michael arrived to the home of Debra and Terry in Midland, Texas. It wasn't too many months later that Terry was transferred to Oklahoma City and we were thrilled to have all our family close by, as Rebecca was living in Ada at that time as well. While they were living in Oklahoma City, Debra and Terry gave us our ninth grandchild, Nathan Dean, born on May 31, 2001. Not much later Terry was transferred to Georgetown, Texas.

During the fifteen years we pastored in Ada, we saw the main building completed and dedicated. We continued on with the youth center, known as "U-turn." To raise money for that project, Mike told the congregation he would cut his hair in a Mohawk cut if they could raise $30,000 in the six weeks leading up to Easter. Well, they raised $60,000 and following Easter services, to the sound of drum rolls, his hairdresser cut his hair as promised – proof was in the Monday paper! When the haircut was completed, Leahna presented her dad with a hat to be worn at all times he would be seen with her...she was not happy about him losing his beautiful head of hair, and neither was I for that matter! But it was for a good cause and it grew back quickly. The building was completed and has been a great blessing not only to the local church, but also to the community.

On July 9, 2002, Rebecca and Jesse Lambert had an elopement/destination wedding in Jamaica! They had advised us of it, but it was impossible for us to go. I will never forget how I cried that day as a friend brought me a bouquet of white roses to my office, "for the mother of the bride." We did get to celebrate them with a reception upon their return. Now all our girls were happily married!

Then on August 25, 2003, our fifth grandson (tenth grandchild), Jordan Andrew (Debra and Terry) was born in Georgetown, Texas. During that time period, we were keeping the highways busy between Branson, Missouri, where Rebecca and Jesse were, and Georgetown, Texas. I have no idea how many miles we drove over those few years, adding even more when Rebecca and Jesse moved to Nashville, Tennessee. But by now you should know…my girls are pretty important to me and time spent with them is a priority!

We also had a day school at the church during a seven-year period but had to close it when the principal moved away and another one was not available. We had Bible Institute classes for much of that time, participated in opportunities to reach out to the needy, maintained a strong income for international mission funds, and established a powerful reputation in the area. Many people were touched in many ways during those fifteen years, and we knew our work was completed upon our resignation and Mike's retirement in January 2006. This time the change was not nearly as difficult, as we would be staying in Ada and be involved in small ways in the church. We were blessed by the gift of an Alaskan cruise as a retirement gift from the church and persuaded our dear friends Harold and Kathy Pinson, to join us.

Brenda and Denny and their family had returned from Ecuador in May of 2002 and immediately came on staff at the church. Mike was anxious for them to adjust to the culture, the area and the people and anticipated them taking the church upon our retirement…and they did. It was such an easy transition for everyone and obviously God's plan. I am so proud of them and the amazing way they have led the congregation in the ensuing years.

On May 24, 2008, we celebrated the wedding of our first grandchild when Michelle married Chad Meadows. They have given me two beautiful little great-granddaughters, Rozalind Michelle and Margot Bailey.

The End of the Dream

*"Often when we lose hope and think this is the
end, God smiles from above and says, 'Relax,
sweetheart, it's just a bend, not the end!'"*

The first few months of his retirement were difficult for Mike, as was to be expected. But then he decided
to start two new careers...farmer and substitute school
teacher! He excelled at both, we had great fresh produce
and Byng (where Leahna taught) and Latta (where Brenda
taught) had a well-liked responsible new substitute teacher. He loved his garden but loved those school kids even
more; they were his new mission field and he spent many
hours in prayer over them. During the following few years
everyone in our family, Mike and I and the four girls, were
all teaching! On December 4, 2009, our sixth grandson and
eleventh grandchild, Asher Michael, was born to Rebecca
and Jesse, in Georgetown, Texas, where they had moved.
Life was good and we looked forward to some fun and travels in the years ahead.

On the evening of December 5, 2009, Mike was
involved in a single vehicle accident on his way home from

Norman after attending an OU girls' basketball game. He missed the deer but hit the telephone pole. He refused going to be seen, saying he was perfectly fine. I was in Georgetown, Texas at the time for the birth of our grandson, Asher. Although I was very concerned about Mike, I had to let him do what he would do. Following that time we began to notice some changes in Mike. He was devastated by the total loss of his most important toy, the little Chevy S-10 he had worked on and souped up, but the changes were physical ones and over the next several months he began to battle a series of set-backs in his health. I greatly admire his courage and faith; he never once complained and kept his good humor to the end. He often quoted, *"My health fails; my spirits droop, yet God remains. He is the strength of my heart, He is mine forever!"* Psalm 73:26. A dear friend and member of our church told me after Mike's passing, "Mike not only taught us the Word, and how to live; he also taught us how to die." This meant so very much to me.

It began in March of 2010 with prostate surgery which had to be repeated a year later, he was hospitalized several times for continual urinary tract infections, was diagnosed with A-fib, developed COPD (although he never smoked a day in his life, but was around second hand smoke all his life, in his growing up years and later on buses and trains in Argentina), had to have hernia surgery, then surgery to place a permanent catheter directly to the bladder. In early 2012 he was diagnosed with thyroid cancer and underwent surgery in June of that year; they were unable to get all the cancer and he never regained enough strength to undergo further treatment. During all this time, commencing shortly after the accident, he had what was thought to be Parkinson's; it was not until several months later that various nurses confided in me that what he had was ALS, or Lou Gehrig's disease.

In April 2012, my mother, Brenda, Denny and I attended the fiftieth anniversary of the Foursquare church in Argentina. This was made possible by Don and Leahna moving Mike to their home, together with all his medical paraphernalia, and Mike's dear friend, Steve Harris, traveling to Ada from California, to care for him during the daytime when Don and Leahna were at work. They all did a fantastic job, and I am so grateful for the opportunity it afforded me to make that trip. I was also needing a break from the job of caretaker. I had started cutting back my hours at work to some extent and still taught at the university.

When I returned, I knew we were facing real problems. Kendra had a big Sweet Sixteen birthday bash in Texas in early July, and Mike insisted on going. It took me three days to pack for the four-day trip and the drive was not an easy one. But we made it and he was so happy. He stayed through the whole party. The highlight for him was when his four girls rolled his wheelchair to the dance floor and danced around him to the Cinderella Waltz...not a dry eye among the some fifty guests, both young and old.

We returned home and a few days later, on Wednesday, July 18th, he had another severe UTI infection. Rebecca and Jesse were visiting us and we tried to get him to the car, but ended up having to call the ambulance. He was immediately put in ICU, with me telling the doctors he had to be out by Saturday for his eldest grandson's wedding. They held out no hope, and by Friday the doctor told me to forget about him being at the wedding. Mike was devastated.

On the day of the wedding, July 21st, I left the hospital around noon to get ready. At 1:00 p.m. the head of ICU called and said if I could get clothes there, she would have Mike ready to go to the wedding as his cardiologist said she would attend the wedding to be there for him. He could be gone only one hour, in a wheelchair, with full oxygen. I got myself somewhat put together and we (my brother and I, who was visiting Mike and there for the wedding) rushed to the hospital. We arrived at the church just in time to be seated with the grandparents with everyone nearly cheering out loud. We had one picture taken with the bride and groom at the end and headed back to the hospital. We rolled him through the ICU doors just as the doctor called the nurse to make sure he had made it back within the allotted hour! Little did we know that would be his last outing. He said that was one of the greatest days of his life as he was able to be a part of Justin's marriage to Katelyn Jones. They have since given me two precious little great-grandsons, Liam Dean and Zion Michael.

On the morning of Saturday, August 4th, his doctor told me I needed to call my family in. We almost lost him that night as the girls and I sat in his ICU room and some other fifty plus people came and went to a conference room the hospital had opened for us. The girls and I were allowed to stay in his ICU room all night. We sang and softly laughed at things we remembered. The next morning he asked where the angels had gone...whether he was seeing angels during the night or thought we were angels, we will never know. By Monday morning he was back in a regular room! Tuesday was his seventy-second birthday. I fixed his favorite meal, chicken, noodles and dumplings. The nurses threw him a little party, and I spent the day reading to him the over a hundred birthday cards he received.

The following week I called a day of fasting and prayer for him, and over five hundred people from around the world responded. At the end of that day, a Byng school bus pulled up to the hospital and the entire girls' basketball team and coaches came into his room, surrounded his bed and prayed. It was truly an unforgettable moment.

On August 17th he was transferred to a rehabilitation center in Norman; but his muscles were too far gone and he was never able to do any rehab. On September 15th I followed the ambulance as it took Mike to our home to be cared for by me and hospice. I am forever grateful to everyone who helped me through that difficult time; the hospice nurses were wonderful, my mother came and stayed with him in the afternoon for three weeks so I could continue to work the necessary hours I needed for insurance. While she was there, all my family came for a weekend and Mike was still able to enjoy them. After my mother left, people like Jim Price, Melvin and Charlotte Harris, Iver and Darleene Hemmerling, came to help in the afternoons. By then I had quit teaching. During those final weeks, Melvin would come to get my car once a week to have it washed and filled with gas, as he knew that was something Mike always did for me!

On October 31st I had to go in to work for a few morning hours and Melvin came to stay with Mike. I called home when leaving work to see what Mike might want for lunch. He wanted a cheeseburger, fries, chili and a chocolate malt from Braum's! I knew he would never eat it but wanted to make him happy; I think he had a couple of bites of each and half of the malt.

The next evening, I called Brenda and Denny to come eat dinner with us as, per usual, I had cooked too much food. When they arrived, Brenda went straight in to see her Daddy, then came back to the kitchen to the cookie drawer. I told her we were about to eat, but she said her Daddy wanted cookies and he was going to have them! He ate little else, we talked a bit after dinner, then he made a joke with Denny and said goodnight. By midnight he was in a coma. I spent that night and most of Friday night awake, watching over him. I finally fell asleep on Saturday mid-morning and slept for about four hours.

He left us on Saturday evening, November 3, 2012 at 8:03 p.m. My life was forever changed, as was that of our entire family. Although I had spent many months already in mourning as I watched his decline, I was not anywhere near ready for the end. Knowing he would probably not make it to our fiftieth wedding anniversary (which he was so greatly anticipating), we had decided on an open house over Thanksgiving weekend to celebrate the date of our engagement. The invitations were addressed and stamped to be mailed, sitting on my dresser. We still had so much more life to live together…but it was not to be.

I have blurred memories of the following days; family, friends, a funeral to plan, phone calls, cards, texts. Then on Wednesday, November 7th, we said our final goodbyes in a celebration of his life attended by nearly four hundred people, standing room only, and more floral arrangements than I have ever seen in any one place. As I went to bed that night, all I could think of was, "What do I do now?" I only had one option…*"But I will sing about your strength, my God, and I will celebrate because of your love. You are my fortress, my place of protection in times of trouble."* Psalm 59:16.

I got up the next day, and the next, and the next... little by little I performed the necessary tasks that need done following a death and kept my head above water. The holidays were a nightmare that I tried to get through without placing too much hardship on my family, but on New Year's Eve at a family get together at Leahna's and Don's, I lost it. It was as if the end of the year made the end of life as I had known it even more intense. I suddenly said, in a voice loud enough for everyone to hear, "I am going to spend next New Year's Eve in Argentina!" I immediately blinked and wondered where in the world that had come from! But I did...

I began putting my financial life in order after the first of the year. I set aside an entire day to call all the doctors, clinics, study centers and hospitals Mike had been to and set up some sort of payment arrangement, knowing that paying the combined amount of some $8,000 was going to be next to impossible, but at least I would offer small payments. After about two hours, I was humbled and grateful to tears – every medical office (except our local hospital) told me not to worry, it was all taken care of, I owed them nothing! I learned that day that God's accounting is nothing like mine! Then there was the amazing way in which the church accepted a property in trust to me until my death, providing funds for what I would have gained had I kept it...more bills covered! And finally, my dear finance friend somehow did a refinance and consolidated my car and house into one very affordable monthly payment.

By March I knew I would be able to live on my income if I retired and put in my resignation effective as of May 1. That was hard – I loved my job, the people, but my health was more important and I had begun to realize how much my health and body had suffered over the months of care-giving. Then I invited my grandson, Justin, and his wife Katelyn to move in with me so they could save money to buy a home. Next I offered to go to Georgetown when Rebecca had the baby she was expecting and be her substitute teacher for six weeks. And then, after thinking it over, I offered to stay the full school year to care of the new baby after she went back to work! And that is how I came to live in Texas for nine months following the birth of Gideon Carlisle to Rebecca and Jesse on August 20, 2013. This gave me seven grandsons and an even dozen grandchildren!

The whole string of decisions I made at that point can only be attributed to God's guidance and the leading of the Holy Spirit. Living with Rebecca and Jesse and the boys gave me the opportunity to be close to Debra and Terry and their family, and the joy of children and young people and a precious new baby, all served to move me forward in the healing process. I would do the same things all over again... in this case, foresight was even better than hindsight! By October I had purchased my ticket to travel to Argentina on December 29th and remain there for two months.

From time to time my daughters and I visit a little country cemetery to honor a man who served his country briefly and spent a lifetime as a soldier of the Cross. Michael's legacy has now been passed down to three generations. God has been so good to our family...His blessings have definitely continued from generation to generation. *"And His mercy is on those who fear Him, from generation to generation."* Luke 1:50.

· XVII ·

But Wait…There's More!

*Sometimes, when we least expect it, we
are granted a new chapter.*

As the weeks passed, I found peace and joy again,
I looked forward to the future…but had no idea what that
future looked like. Everyone, friends and family alike, were
very caring and thoughtful as I got back up on my feet. Our
long-time friend, Steve Harris, had lost his wife the year
before Mike passed, and he had been encouraging me with
a card from time to time and wise words on moving forward, remembering Mike with me on birthdays and holidays. At some point we began to share phone chats and
more encouragement.

Steve's father passed away in September (2013), and
Steve mentioned he was very tired after working hard on
clearing his dad's home and such. I suggested he take a vacation and invited him to spend Thanksgiving in Oklahoma
with all our clan, plus he had relatives there as well who
would welcome him to visit. He called to tell me the dates
wouldn't work, but asked what I thought about him coming

to Texas for a visit in early December. I said sure…come on. We would all love to see him. Then he threw me a curve – he called and wanted me to ask all my girls if it was OK for him to come for a visit. I thought that was strange and not at all necessary, but I asked them, and they all thought it was a good idea. He could stay at Debra and Terry's home.

And that was the beginning of the next chapter of my life! He came for a week, we enjoyed long visits, a movie, a day at the River Walk in San Antonio, some drives around the area, most of the time under the chaperoning of baby Gideon! The day he left I felt strangely lonesome, and within a few days realized I missed him. But I needed to move on and make final preparations for my Argentine adventure. Steve did mention at some point, "Now don't go down there and fall in love with some rich Argentine gaucho!" We still have a good laugh about that from time to time!

My time in Argentina was as perfect as it could be. I saw everyone I wanted to see, traveled to several of my favorite spots, ministered in various churches, and spent a lot of quality time with my other "kid," Florence.

Interestingly, the Lord urged me to ask forgiveness wherever I went, whether one-on-one or in church settings. I had no clue what this was about, as I have never been one to hold grudges, unforgiveness, nor did I know what I was asking forgiveness for…but I obeyed. I got some funny looks, laughs, and questions as to what I thought I needed to ask forgiveness for; I just kept being obedient. I even took the giant step of visiting Mr. PDP (remember him?) and asked for forgiveness. It wasn't until near the end of my trip that it was made clear: the Foursquare church in Argentina had gone though a very difficult time and, as tends to happen in this type of crisis, people had taken sides in the matter. When I began asking forgiveness for seemingly nothing, it made many realize they truly did have reason to seek forgiveness and new bridges were built in relationships. I look back on those two months with nothing but joy and precious memories. I hated to leave, but knew I needed to head stateside and see what was ahead.

Not wanting to seem intrusive, I didn't call Steve until I had been back several days; and when I did, he was pretty miffed that I had not called at once when I returned! After a few weeks, I planned a week to go to California and we enjoyed a great time together...still quite platonic. But the phone calls became more frequent and we both knew something more was brewing. I moved back to Ada in June of 2014 and had decided I would begin to slowly start getting rid of things with the intention of selling the house and down-sizing within a year or so.

In one of our many conversations, Steve and I settled on meeting up in Indiana in October where he would be visiting his sister; I was going to see my brother in Illinois and wanted to drive to Indiana to visit Mike's Uncle Skeeter (I am so glad I did as he passed away not too long after that). We thought it was time to do some serious talking.

Surrounded by so many of Steve's relatives, it was difficult to find any time for our conversation. But finally, on the morning I was to drive back to Gerry's, we went to breakfast at Bruner's Restaurant. As Steve put it, "I guess you would like to know where you stand!" Yes, I did! By the time breakfast was over, we confessed our friendship had blossomed and love was in the air. As we went to the car to take him back to his sister's and me to drive to Illinois, he took the opportunity to seal the deal with a kiss!

I had already planned on spending three weeks with my mother over the Christmas holidays, and now planned to leave a week earlier and spend time in California. Our kids were all on board, and as one of my daughters later put it, the whole thing was God-orchestrated. Steve placed a promise ring on my finger on that December visit and we settled on a wedding in April. I enjoyed a wonderful time with my mother, and she was delighted that I would not be alone and would be taken care. Besides, she had always thought Steve was great since the many years before when she first met him.

I guess you might say the rest is history. Steve flew to Ada in January and gave me an engagement ring, and I began seriously downsizing and preparing for a pretty drastic change. As much work as it was and hard to get everything done, the Lord sent me a great help through a work friend (Geraldine Anderson), who worked hard right along beside me. Then another dear friend (Lisa Daniel) ended up being my "real estate agent," recommending my house to a young couple we both knew. Then to help even more, Eliana came for a week to give me another great boost. And finally, it was done…garage sale, furniture sales, moving the things I was keeping into storage, and initial signing on the sale of the house.

April 18, 2015 was a beautiful spring day in Ada, Oklahoma, and our wedding day went off without a hitch, with Denny and Steve's brother, Mark, performing a tremendously meaningful ceremony, surrounded by all our family and many friends. The next day we attended church to be a part of great-granddaughter Margot's baby dedication and left for California that afternoon after locking up my Ada home for the last time. We enjoyed a leisurely road trip along Route 66, part of the old as well as the new, and arrived at my new home on April 24th.

We can honestly say that we moved right into our life together without any complications. Of course we had the great advantage of having been friends and known each other for many years and had many mutual friends and ministry experiences. Jesse and Rebecca drove my U-Haul out for me following the July Ada Connection – joining two households into a home smaller than I had has presented some challenges, but we have managed quite well.

I already knew the pastor of the church Steve was a part of in Hesperia and have been blessed to enjoy a wonderful relationship with Bill and Denise Burnett. Soon I had made new friends and Steve and I had a little group we could hang out with and depend on when needed.

We were enjoying our life, preparing for a trip to Hawaii with Steve's family, when suddenly we faced a big issue. I went in for a doctor's visit, mainly to get my foot in her door anticipating the day I might need a doctor. She asked me how I was and I responded I felt a bit tired and occasionally out of breath, but had decided that was normal since I had been a care-taker to a very ill husband for many months, then had cared for a newborn grandson for a few months, traveled out of the country for two months, emptied out and sold a house and gotten rid of many items, packed up for a move, planned a wedding and moved to California...I had a right to be tired. But she wanted me to have a cardiac work up, just to be sure. Well, a large mass was found in my heart that would require open-heart surgery as soon as could be arranged.

We went ahead with our trip and then into medical mode immediately upon our return. After more testing and pre-surgery prep, surgery was performed on October 30, 2015. Although I insisted my girls not come, I guess they voted and Debra came to be here during the week of surgery and Leahna the week after – which worked out fine, as Debra and Steve stayed down at Tammy and John's while I was in the hospital and ate out, and Leahna cooked for us when she came as I was home. Of course, you all know how much Debra likes to cook...! I can honestly say, I felt absolutely no fear during that entire time. *"I will give you rest – everything will be fine for you."* Exodus 33:14. I was more concerned for Steve, who had already lost one wife with heart issues, and about my family, who I knew would be greatly concerned. I thank God for His care and healing – I don't even have much of a scar to show for it!

On February 19, 2018, my precious mother went to her heavenly home. I am so grateful to Steve for insisting I go to visit a week earlier than I had planned. That allowed me to be at her side during her last days. It is an interesting thing when you no longer have either of your parents – it's like you move up to a new position and feel a heavier load for your family. My mother was an amazing woman of God, a blessing to thousands, faithful to the very end to her calling, and a fervent prayer warrior. I know she prayed for my family constantly; I now feel the need to ramp up my prayers for them. I miss her terribly and look forward to a great family reunion someday.

This second, unexpected chapter, has been a very happy one. A few months after we were married a friend (who is a Christian counselor) asked what had been our most difficult problem of adaptation. We looked at each other trying to think of any problem we had, then Steve responded, "You know, between us we do have over one hundred years of marriage experience…we ought to have it down pretty good!" I am content in my new surroundings, Steve is so very loving and caring, and we are greatly enjoying doing life together. Our love is very special. Travels, family times, church friends, times of reminiscing and – of course – watching old westerns, all keep us entertained. Our families have all given us so much love and acceptance and our (currently) forty-two member clan has merged well. The bonus family I have gained, Tammy and John Shaw and their children, Janaea, Brittany, Jeremy and great-grandchildren, Taylor and Gramm; Steve and Terra Harris and their daughters, Kelsey and husband Marcel Valenzuela, Courtney, and Kiersten and husband Steven Delben, are all very dear to me. I look forward to growing old with this wonderful man God has given me. God has been very, VERY good to me…I have been doubly blessed! As I have sung and said my whole life, "I don't know what the future holds, but I know who holds the future." And that is all I need to know!

· XVIII ·

Reflections...

*"This is my story, this is my song, Praising
my Savior all the day long!"*

As I come to the end of my story...at least so far... I
look back with awe at everything I have experienced in my
life. I have learned how everything can change in the blink
of an eye. But I no longer worry; God never blinks!

By the time we left Argentina, we had watched the
fulfillment of a vision become a reality. Upon returning to
the United States in December of 1990, Mike was anxious
to see if the same concept would work in a totally different
cultural setting. Upon establishing the Foursquare Church
in Ada, Oklahoma, each step has been reproduced and as of
this writing continues strong under the leadership of Denny
and Brenda. Although methods, finances, and cultures may
change, God's initial plan for going into all the world and
making disciples remains the same!

Following our retirement from senior church leadership, we also continued to pour into the lives of young
ministers in various parts of the USA, both Foursquare and
from other denominations. I still do.

When at times I am feeling a bit sorry for myself, and think I cannot keep up the fast pace I have often been thrown into, I am ashamed to admit I have found myself basking in a pretty deep pit of self-pity. It is then I feel as though someone slaps me up side the face, and says, "Woman, your worst day is a good day! All your girls, sons-in-law, grandchildren and close family members love and serve the Lord. You have a happy marriage. Your needs are met. What more do you want?" It is at those times that I undergo an immediate attitude adjustment! I have learned to not cry because an era is over, but to smile because it happened.

Through the years I have enormously enjoyed singing with my girls; I have heard raindrops on rooftops, waves lapping on the shore, the cooing and laughter of babies, wind chimes, the songs of birds, crickets on a warm summer evening. The sweet sound of my grandchildren saying they love me, the sound of laughter, giggling, talking and singing together of my daughters...these are the sounds of my favorite things.

I rejoice at good news from friends, feel sorrow at the loss of dear ones passing away, joy at the birth of a new baby born into my extended family, and horror at some of the world news. But there is, has always been, and will always be one constant: God is still on the throne! I choose to serve Him, love people and allow the joy of the Lord to always be my strength. I can honestly say I would not make any major changes to my life. Yes, I have made mistakes, messed up, done some stupid things along the way, but these have all formed the life I have lived and God has used even the dumb stuff for my good. I plan to live for as long as I live! *"You are old and advanced in years, and there remains yet very much land to possess."* Joshua 13:1.

I truly have led a many-faceted life...still do! I could brag about all the places I have traveled to, or about my education, which includes a Certificate of Bible and Christian Education Studies from the Foursquare Bible Institute in Honduras; Bilingual Secretarial graduate from Alpha Academy in Honduras; Certificate of Public and Written Translation from the School of Language in Guadalajara, Mexico; Standard Ministerial Studies at L.I.F.E. Bible College and Bachelor of Ministry in World Missions from the College for Global Deployment in Vancouver, Washington, or about the many ministry and work positions I have filled. Don't get me wrong, I am grateful for all that.

But by far my highest honors are being the proud mother of four unbelievably amazing daughters, mother-in-law to my four boys...sons-in-love, and grandmother to the 12 most wonderful grandchildren in the world, and two loving grandchildren-in-love, my four (so far!) precious great grands and adding fantastic grand-kids-in-law as time goes by, and now the bonus family I have in Steve's children, grandchildren and great-grandchildren. Not too long ago on a recent visit to my kids, my girls and several of the grandkids were drinking mate around the dining room table, singing silly songs, laughing and having so much fun together...you could just sense the love oozing in the house! I was cooking in the kitchen and listening, and I just teared all up at how blessed I am that they all love to be together, have so much fun together, and enjoy each other so much. I am so blessed and deeply grateful!

Brenda Michelle, Leahna Jeanelle, Debra Lynelle and Rebecca Ruth, when this story is all that is left of me and I move to my heavenly home, never doubt that you were loved beyond measure, that you made your Daddy and me the proudest people ever, and you have made me the happiest woman that ever lived. You are my forever treasures and I anticipate all of eternity enjoying your smiles, laughter, songs and acts of love and kindness. Yes, I do love you and your families more than words can ever express. If I had to choose between loving you and breathing, I would use my last breath telling you how much I love you!

Years ago, as a child of ten, I heard something that I wrote in my Bible: "Only one life, will soon be past; only what's done for Christ will last." I am the only person on earth that can make use of my God-given abilities; I always try to do every day all that can be done by me on that day. And I try to take time often to celebrate my successes – even the little ones.

So in closing, I just want to encourage you…no matter what feelings you may have about today, keep in mind that this day is the Lord's day – finish it well and be done with it! You will have the peace of knowing you have done what you could. And always remember, the best is yet to come…always. Tomorrow is a new beginning!

"O God, You have taught me from my youth;
and to this day I declare your wondrous works.
Now also, when I am old and gray headed,
O God, do not forsake me,
until I declare your strength to this generation!"
Psalm 71:17-18

My parents, circa 1943.

Me at three months.

Favorite coat, made by Grandma (three years old).

SPECIAL SERVICES

with the

GURNEY GOSPEL GROUP

Starting Sun., Oct. 14

CONTINUING EVERY NIGHT
(Except Monday)

EVANGELISTS
EDWIN and VONITTA GURNEY

ENJOY OLD-FASHIONED SINGING DIRECTED BY SONG LEADER EDWIN GURNEY, SOLOIST AND RADIO ARTIST. HEAR OLD-FASHIONED GOSPEL PREACHING BY ONE OF AMERICA'S OUTSTANDING LADY EVANGELISTS, VONITTA GURNEY.

Featuring...

Six Year Old Soloist

Lolita Gurney

Her singing before large audiences across America and Canada, and over radio stations has stirred the hearts of many. Be sure and hear her this week.

Foursquare Community Church of Woodburn

REV. ARTHUR GOBLE, Pastor
1197 E. Lincoln Street

"Sweetheart of Revival"

First church and home in Honduras.

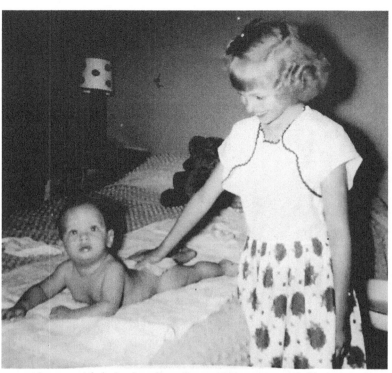

Above, with baby brother, Gerry. Below, special Christmas.

Family picture, including Judy.

With Harris Family, December 1961; Victorville, CA.

The Frederick Family, circa 1981.

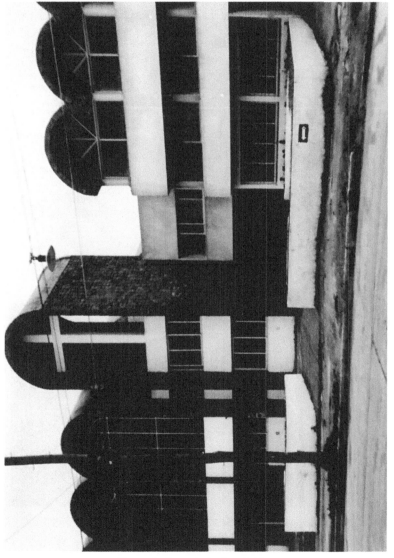

Central Church in San Isidro.

With first ordained minister from Toba tribe, Northern
Argentina.

Mike and me, circa 1993.

With my four daughters.

With Steve and the whole Frederick-Harris Clan
on our wedding day.

Steve and me, 2015.

Page 39
Page 121
Page 133

Made in the USA
Coppell, TX
30 December 2020